English Insights 1

Student's Book

Helen Stephenson

Jane Bailey

Contents

2

CONTENTS

1 ⊙*S1* **Read and listen to four friends. Which of them have got the same favourite school subjects or hobbies?**

2 Answer the questions about Lauren and Jack.

1 How old is Lauren?
2 What did the hockey team win last year?
3 What does she want to do this year?
4 Where does Jack live?
5 What does he do at weekends?
6 When did he join a folk group?

3 Write questions about Reem and Lee.

1 Where / be / Reem / from?
2 When / she / move / to England?
3 What / she / do / on Saturdays?
4 Where / be / Lee / born?
5 What / be / his ambition?
6 What / he / do / last year?

4 Work in pairs. Ask and answer the questions in Exercise 3.

66 Hello. My name's Lauren. My mum is from Ireland, so I'm half-Irish. I'm 15 and I'm in Year 10. My favourite subjects are PE and biology. I love sports and I play in the school hockey team. Last year, we won the girls' hockey tournament. I like water sports too. This year, I want to join the rowing club in my town. **99**

66 Hi. I'm Jack. I live next door to Lauren. We both enjoy playing tennis in the park at weekends. My favourite subjects at school are PE and music. I play the violin and the piano. I started the violin when I was six. Two years ago, I joined a folk group. This month we're taking part in a folk music festival. **99**

66 My name's Reem and I'm in the same class as Jack. I'm Lebanese and my family moved to England when I was seven. My hobbies are reading and acting. I love reading detective stories and thrillers, and I go to the theatre on Saturdays. I want to be a writer when I leave school. **99**

66 I'm Lee. I was born in England, but my dad's family is from China. My favourite school subjects are maths and science. My ambition is to go to university and study to be a doctor. I love football and last year I joined the school football club. We play matches against other schools on Saturdays. **99**

Home and school

GRAMMAR
Learn about the present simple and present continuous uses of verbs, and verbs without a continuous form.

SKILLS
Read about teenagers living in the UK, schools, and studying in the Australian outback.

Listen to a student talking about her school, and a teacher talking about his school.

Write a personal email.

COMMUNICATE!
Make greetings and introductions.

VOCABULARY
Learn words for places in homes and schools, school subjects, and adjectives to describe personality.

Work with positive and negative adjectives, and *do* and *make*.

1 Work in pairs. Look at the photo of a houseboat. How many rooms do you think it has got? Use words from the Vocabulary box.

2 ⊙ 1.1 Listen to three conversations. Where are the people? Write the numbers (1–3) next to three places in the Vocabulary box.

3 Work in pairs. Write a list of things in your homes. Can you use every letter of the alphabet?

▶ *A – armchair, B – bath, C – cupboard …*

4 Work in pairs. Take turns to describe a room in your house and to guess your partner's room.

Homes	
bathroom	garden
bedroom	hall
bungalow	house
dining room	kitchen
flat	living room
floor	study
garage	toilet

Reading and listening

1 Read the introduction to the webpage. Tick the things you think the new arrivals will talk about.

| families | food | friends | houses | people |
| schools | teachers | the weather | | |

2 ⊙ *1.2* Read and listen to the webpage. Check your answers to Exercise 1.

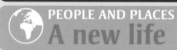

🏠 HOME   🐾 ANIMALS   🌍 **PEOPLE AND PLACES**   🏃 ACTIVITIES   🎥 VIDEOS

PEOPLE AND PLACES
A new life

Every year, more than 26,000 children arrive in Britain. We ask some new arrivals what they like best about their new lives and what's different from home.

Daisy and Luke, the USA

My brother and I like living here in Brighton, it's cool! My brother loves the British accent: 'tomato' and 'banana'. Everybody here is very polite too. But we don't understand all your strange words – we say 'yard' not 'garden' and 'apartment' not 'flat', you know? We have a big bungalow with a pool in the USA. Here we live in a three-storey house. Our bedrooms are on the top floor and the kitchen is on the ground floor. It seems a long way! My brother is too lazy to come downstairs for breakfast. The food is better here. There's Indian, Chinese and Thai. At home we eat too much fast food. I hate fast food. Well, OK, I don't hate it. But it's so unhealthy, you know?

Yosuf, Egypt

I don't know anybody from Egypt here in Manchester, but I'm lucky because the English boy next door is my age. He's very friendly and kind. At home we live in a block of flats, but here we have a house. My new school is really big. I'm always late for my classes. The teachers understand, they're very patient. And they don't give much homework. I prefer English schools – at home, the teachers seem a bit strict and serious. There are a lot of rules. Here students go out of school and buy pizza or burgers at lunchtime. We can't do that in Egypt.

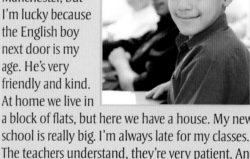

Shruti, India

It's too cold and windy here in Cambridge! I hate doing sports outside in winter. The teacher at my new school is very serious about sports, but I'm not competitive. I prefer science and maths. I love the maths class because the teacher is really funny. I want to go to the Science Museum in London, but London is so big and the people seem unfriendly. We're from a small village in India. I know all the people and places. In London, I need a map!

CHECK IT!

3 Read the webpage again. Are the sentences true or false?

1 Daisy and Luke want to go home to the USA.

2 Yosuf's new life is different from his life in Egypt.

3 Shruti likes her maths teacher.

4 Read the webpage again. Answer the questions.

1 What does Luke love about Britain?

2 What don't Daisy and Luke understand?

3 Who does Yosuf know in Britain?

4 What does Yosuf like about Britain?

5 Why does Shruti hate doing sports outside?

6 Which subjects does Shruti prefer?

Grammar: present simple and verbs without a continuous form

5 Look at the examples (1–3). Match them with the meanings (a–c).

1 We eat too much fast food.

2 I want to go to the Science Museum.

3 We live in a block of flats.

a a regular habit

b a permanent state

c a feeling or thought

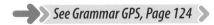 See Grammar GPS, Page 124

6 Find these verbs in the webpage. Write them in the correct place in the table. If you don't know their meaning, use a dictionary to help you.

like	love	understand	live	seem
eat	prefer	go out	need	

regular habits	buy, give, _____ , _____
permanent states	have, _____
feelings and thoughts	hate, know, want, _____ , _____ , _____ , _____ , _____ , _____ ,

 We can use *have* or *have got* to talk about possession, illnesses and relationships, with no difference in meaning.

See Grammar GPS, Page 124

7 Complete the sentences with the correct form of six of the verbs in the box.

hate	know	like	love	need
prefer	seem	understand	want	

1 It's my first day. I don't _____ anybody in my class.

2 London _____ very big to me.

3 It's my friend's birthday soon. He _____ an MP3 player.

4 My spelling is terrible. I _____ a dictionary.

5 I _____ Chinese food to Indian food.

6 My grandfather doesn't _____ English.

 Verbs for thoughts and feelings do not usually have a present continuous form. But remember! After *hate / like / love / prefer*, we still use the verb + *-ing*.
I like reading. I prefer reading to watching TV.

8 Work in pairs. Complete the conversations with the verbs in the box in Exercise 7. Then practise. Take turns.

1 **A:** Do you _____ a sandwich?
   B: No thanks, I'm not hungry.

2 **A:** Do you _____ living in Britain?
   B: Yes, but I _____ the USA.

3 **A:** Can you do this maths homework?
   B: No, I _____ a calculator.

4 **A:** Our new PE teacher _____ a bit serious.
   B: I know!

Vocabulary: personality adjectives

9 Choose the correct option.

1 My friend is so *funny / friendly*. She makes us laugh a lot.

2 Our new neighbours are *lazy / kind*. They always help us.

3 My brother always wants to win. He's too *polite / competitive*.

4 There are lots of rules in our school. It's very *strict / patient*.

5 My grandfather never laughs. He's very *serious / lucky*.

Working with words: positive adjective ▶ negative adjective

10 Look at the examples. Then find another adjective starting with *un* in the webpage.

My neighbour is friendly.
The people in London seem unfriendly.

See Working with words, Page 116

Speaking

11 Write the names of people you know for each adjective in Exercise 9.

▶ *serious - my uncle Bill*

12 Work in pairs. Tell your partner about six people from Exercise 11. Take turns.

A: *My uncle Bill is a bit serious. He never smiles or laughs.*

 If you have time
Which is the odd one out in each list? Why? Write more lists for a partner.
1 apartment chair flat house
2 armchair bed microwave sofa
3 bath shower sink TV
4 door kitchen roof wall

Speaking

1 Put the words in the box into two groups: *school subjects* and *places in a school*. Can you add any more words to your lists?

> art room   canteen   chemistry
> food technology   geography   gym   hall
> history   IT room   language laboratory
> library   maths   music room   PE
> sports field   technology room   workshop

2 Work in pairs. Describe what you're doing and guess the place. Take turns.

A: *I'm listening to a conversation in French.*

B: *The language laboratory.*

A day at Central High School

Mark Jones

It's only my third week at my new school and I love it! Today's Friday – the best day of the week at Central High.

Why? Well, my first class on Fridays is music. I'm learning to play the trumpet this year and I love it! I practise every lunchtime in the music room because I'm not very good at the moment – I make a terrible noise!

Then we have maths. We do a test every Friday, but I'm quite good at maths so it's OK. After maths, we have English. It's probably my favourite subject. I'm in the English class now – we're doing a project called 'A day at Central High School' for the school website. It's very quiet at the moment because everybody's writing their projects. I can hear the class next door. They're reading aloud from Shakespeare's *Julius Caesar*. Actually, that's a good play for our school because there aren't many parts in it for girls! Outside, on the sports field, the rugby team is practising for the match on Saturday. Mr Fleming, the PE teacher, is shouting at them. Our school's brilliant at rugby, actually. We often win the Schools Cup.

Friday afternoons are great because we can choose our classes. This term I'm doing food technology. We make some fantastic dishes – spaghetti bolognese, chocolate cake, biscuits! Who says cooking is just for girls?!

Reading and listening

3 Look at the photos. Find three things that are the same or different in your school.

4 🔘 **1.3** Read and listen to the text. Which photo is Central High School? How do you know?

5 Read the text again. Why does Mark like Fridays? Find three reasons.

a

b

Listening

6 ⊙**1.4** **Listen to Suzi Wade, a student at an all-girls school. What does Suzi talk about?**

a The places at Oaklands School.

b Her favourite subjects and teachers.

c The reasons all-girls schools are better.

7 ⊙**1.4** **Listen again. Complete the sentences with** *Girls* **or** *Boys***.**

1 _____ are more responsible.

2 _____ are better at languages.

3 _____ are good at making things.

Speaking

8 **Work in pairs. Do you agree with the sentences in Exercise 7? Why? / Why not? Now discuss these statements.**

1 Boys are more competitive.

2 Girls are more responsible.

3 Girls get better exam results.

Working with words: *do* and *make*

9 **Look at the examples. Then read the text quickly and find other examples of** *make* **and** *do***.**

We're doing a project.

We're making a cake.

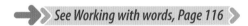 See Working with words, Page 116

Grammar: present simple and present continuous

10 Underline **the present continuous verbs and** circle **the present simple verbs in the text.**

11 **Write** *present simple* **or** *present continuous* **for each use.**

1 an activity in progress at or around the time of speaking

_____

2 a regular or repeated activity

_____

3 a state or feeling

_____

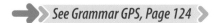 See Grammar GPS, Page 124

12 **Complete the sentences with the present simple or present continuous form of the verbs.**

▶ This term in chemistry, we _are learning_ about metals. (learn)

1 Our class usually _____ gymnastics on Mondays. (do)

2 We _____ rugby this term. (play)

3 'What's that terrible noise?' 'It's John. He _____ the violin.' (practise)

4 My friend loves reading. She _____ two books every week. (read)

5 That's another goal! We _____ by three goals to one now. (win)

6 We _____ a model of our school in art at the moment. (make)

13 **Write the correct form of the verbs: present simple or present continuous.**

This year, Mark (**1** study) _____ ten subjects. He (**2** have) _____ about five hours of lessons every day. His best subjects (**3** be) _____ technology and IT. In technology, he (**4** make) _____ a robot. And in IT this term, they (**5** learn) _____ about virtual reality. Mark (**6** enjoy) _____ school, but he (**7** not / like) _____ homework. He (**8** get) _____ homework most days. He (**9** do) _____ his homework in his bedroom and he (**10** listen) _____ to music at the same time.

14 **Rewrite the sentences in Exercise 13 about you.**

▶ *This year, I'm studying …*

Speaking

15 **Write questions about the information in Exercise 14.**

▶ *How many subjects are you studying this year?*

16 **Work in pairs. Ask and answer your questions from Exercise 15.**

A: *How many subjects are you studying this year?*

B: *Nine. What about you?*

A: *I'm doing ten.*

Reading and listening

1 ⊙*1.5* **Read and listen to the dialogue. Who is the man in the photo?**

2 <u>Underline</u> these ways of introducing and greeting people in the dialogue.

This is …

Let me introduce …

How do you do?

Lauren:	Hi, Jack. How are you?
Jack:	I'm fine. And you?
Lauren:	I'm great! I had a fantastic time in Ireland.
Jack:	Do you want to come to the park for a game of tennis?
Lauren:	Yes, but my cousin and her parents are here at the moment. They're staying with us for a few days.
Jack:	That's OK. Your cousin can come too.
Lauren:	OK. Why don't you come in first, and meet Erin and my uncle? My aunt is out shopping with my mum, but you can meet her later.
Jack:	OK. Sure.
Lauren:	Erin. This is my friend, Jack. He lives next door.
Erin:	Hello, Jack.
Jack:	Hello, Erin. Nice to meet you.
Erin:	Nice to meet you too.
Lauren:	Let me introduce my uncle, Professor Taggart.
Jack:	How do you do, Professor?
Erin's dad:	How do you do, Jack? Call me Mr Taggart. I'm only Professor Taggart when I'm working.
Jack:	OK. Pleased to meet you, Mr Taggart.
Erin's dad:	And I'm very pleased to meet you, Jack. I hear you play a good game of tennis.
Jack:	Well … I play a lot of tennis in the summer, so I'm not bad. I'm better than Lauren, anyway!
Lauren:	I'm not sure about that! Erin's brilliant at tennis and I'm learning a lot from her. We practise every day.
Erin:	I've got an idea. Why don't I play Jack first? Then we can see who's the best!
Lauren:	Yes, let's do that.
Erin:	OK. Let's go, then. Bye, Dad.
Jack:	Goodbye, Mr Taggart.
Lauren:	Bye, Uncle Sean. See you later!
Erin's dad:	Bye. Have a good time!

3 ⊙*1.6* **Listen and repeat the *Useful expressions*. Focus on your intonation.**

Useful expressions

Informal: for greeting and introducing people your own age, or people you know well

A: Hi, Jack. How are you?   A: This is my friend, Jack.
B: I'm fine. And you?   B: Nice to meet you, Jack.
A: I'm great!   C: Nice to meet you too.

Formal: for introducing people in a polite way
A: Let me introduce my uncle, Professor Taggart.
B: How do you do, Professor?
C: How do you do, Jack? Call me Mr Taggart.
B: Pleased to meet you, Mr Taggart.

CHECK IT!

4 ○ *1.7* **Listen to four statements twice. Choose the best response (a, b or c).**

1 a Hello. Nice to meet you.
b I'm fine. And you?
c Hi.

2 a How are you?
b I'm fine, thanks.
c How do you do?

3 a Pleased to meet you, Mrs Smith.
b Hello, Grandma.
c Call me Shirley.

4 a Hello, Lauren. Nice to meet you.
b Nice to meet you, too.
c I'm fine, thanks.

Writing: a personal email

1 Read Lee's email to his brother and answer the questions.

1 Why does Lee like his teacher?
2 Why has he got a lot of homework?
3 Why is his football team practising hard at the moment?

2 Underline *and, because, but* and *so* in the email.

3 Complete the sentences with *and, because, but* or *so*.

1 I don't know many people in my class, _____ they all seem very nice.
2 I meet my best friend at 8 a.m. _____ we walk to school together.
3 I'm on the school team this year, _____ I go to football practice every lunchtime.
4 Everybody seems more serious _____ we've got exams this year.

4 Make notes about your first week back at school. Include information about your studies, your teachers and your hobbies. Say what you are doing at the moment.

Then write an email to a friend or a relation. Remember to join your sentences with *and, because, but* and *so*.

Pronunciation: weak form /ə/

5 ○ *1.8* **Listen to these sentences from the dialogue. Is the underlined word stressed (S) or unstressed (U)?**

1 I had <u>a</u> fantastic time in Ireland!
2 Pleased <u>to</u> meet you, Mr Taggart.
3 How do <u>you</u> do, Professor?
4 Erin's brilliant <u>at</u> tennis!

6 ○ *1.8* **Listen to the sentences again. Words which don't give important information are not stressed and the vowel sound is weak: /ə/. Practise saying the sentences.**

Speaking

7 Work in groups of three. Write dialogues for each situation. Then practise your dialogues. Take turns in each role.

1 You go to your friend's party and greet him /her.
Your friend introduces you to his / her brother / sister.
Roles: (**a**) you
(**b**) your friend
(**c**) your friend's brother / sister

2 You're shopping with your mum / dad. You meet your new teacher in the street. Introduce the teacher to your mum / dad.
Roles: (**a**) you
(**b**) your mum / dad
(**c**) your teacher

To:	\<Cheng\>
From:	\<Lee\>
Subject:	First week at school

Hi Cheng,

How are you? How's university? I'm back at school, of course! I've got a new teacher, Miss Jones. She's an excellent teacher, but she's really strict! She teaches science and she's brilliant at explaining new ideas. I like her because she's friendly and she doesn't shout.

We've got a lot of exams this year, so I have to do homework every night. I also practise with the school football club twice a week. We're practising really hard at the moment because we've got a big match against a very good team next month and we need to improve!

Mum's calling me for dinner, so I must go now. I think we're having chicken with chips! My favourite!
See you soon,
Lee

Australia online: the world's largest classroom

Reading

1 Work in pairs. Look at the photos. What can you see?

2 🔘 1.9 Read the text. What is 'the world's largest classroom'?

Culture

Australia

The Australian outback is one of the most isolated parts of the world. It covers a huge area of more than 1.5 million square kilometres. The towns are hundreds of kilometres apart. Most people live on sheep farms or cattle stations. Outback children are different from children from urban areas. They study at home and don't attend traditional schools. Many of them work on the family farm from an early age. They learn to ride horses and to survive in difficult situations. They are more mature and better at studying alone than city children. They are also good at organising their work.

Young outback children study with the School of the Air and older students can enrol at a School of Distance Education (SODE). About 15 per cent of the students are Aborigines. In the past, students and teachers used two-way radio. The name 'School of the Air' comes from that time. Today, teachers give lessons by satellite and use an electronic whiteboard. Most students have a satellite dish and a computer with a webcam. They log in to classes in real time and can see their teacher on their computer screen. The teacher can demonstrate skills in science, music, art, PE, drama or poetry. Students can also talk to each other and to the teacher.

As well as attending classes, students also have to do coursework and exams, and younger children have an online school assembly once a week. In addition, there are opportunities for students to meet. Three or four times a year, students travel to the nearest centre to take part in different activities, such as sports week and school excursions.

3 Read the text again and answer the questions.

1 Where do children in the outback live?

2 How are outback students different?

3 How do they study?

4 When do students meet?

4 Find words in the text that mean the same as the underlined words.

1 Some of the farms are for <u>cows</u>.

2 Outback children don't <u>go to</u> normal schools.

3 Students <u>connect online</u> to their classes.

4 Every week there's <u>a meeting of the whole school</u>.

5 The students go on school <u>trips</u> to interesting places.

Listening

5 🔘 *1.10* Listen to a teacher from an Australian School of Distance Education (SODE). Are the sentences true or false?

1 Michael Sheen teaches science.

2 He teaches very young children.

3 He does experiments in front of a large class.

4 The students don't listen to his lessons.

5 The students are not good at working on their own.

6 SODE students often get better results than students at an ordinary school.

6 🔘 *1.10* Michael Sheen talks about the similarities and differences between teaching in a regular school and teaching at an SODE. Listen again and complete the sentences.

Similarities

1 There's a lot of ....

2 We prepare our ....

Differences

3 The classroom is ....

4 He can't see the ....

Technology and English
Languages and the internet

1 Work in pairs. Discuss these questions with your partner.

1 How do people use computers to communicate with each other?

2 Which languages do most people use?

2 Read the article and check your answers.

Modern technology helps people to stay in touch. In the past, people wrote letters or sent telegrams, and long distance telephone calls were very expensive. Today, people use computers to communicate with friends or family who live far away. Almost everybody uses email these days and internet phone connections, such as Skype, are becoming more popular every day. Young people, in particular, enjoy using webcams and keeping in touch with their friends.

There are one billion internet users in the world today and about one third log on in English. That's because web technology started in the United States and most webpages are in English. In addition, over 60 per cent of people in the UK, the USA, Canada and Australia are online. However, more and more Chinese people connect to the Internet every day. Today there are more than 160 million people logging on in Chinese and experts predict that the number of users will continue to increase. Other internet languages that are growing rapidly are Spanish and Arabic.

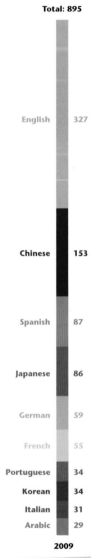

Total: 895

Language	Users (millions)
English	327
Chinese	153
Spanish	87
Japanese	86
German	59
French	55
Portuguese	34
Korean	34
Italian	31
Arabic	29

Top ten languages used on the Internet: by number of users (millions)

2009

3 Why do you think that the number of Chinese, Spanish and Arabic internet users is growing quickly?

Project Write about your school. Describe the building, the classrooms, subjects, other activities, etc. What are the students and teachers good at? Include some photos.

Reading

HOW TO...

identify detailed information
- Read the text quickly.
- Read the true or false statements. <u>Underline</u> the key words – the important information – in each statement.
- Read the text again and <u>underline</u> the parts which match the key words.
- Decide if each statement is true or false.

Important! Remember that different words often express the same idea.

1 Read the text quickly. Then read the statements. <u>Underline</u> the key words in each statement.

Summerhill School is a private school in England. Students live at the school during term time. The school is very different from a traditional school because the students decide how to spend their time. They can go to classes – or they can do what they want. The art room is always open and many students spend time there. Students in a class are not always the same age. Students who are good at a subject study with older students. All the students can take part in school meetings and make important decisions about the school.

1 The children eat and sleep at the school.
2 Summerhill School is a traditional school.
3 Students always go to classes.
4 Students make decisions at school meetings.

CHECK IT!

2 Read the text again.
Which parts match the key words in the statements? Decide if each statement is true (T) or false (F).

HOW TO...

complete the sentences
- Read the sentences carefully, and <u>underline</u> the same information in the text.
- Then think of one word to write in each gap. The word is often a similar word or an opposite word to the one in the text.

CHECK IT!

3 Complete the sentences with one word.

1 The art room .... closes.
2 There are often students of .... ages in the same class.

Language response

HOW TO...

choose the appropriate linguistic response
- Read the responses (a, b and c), and decide what situation the person is in and what kind of statement the other person is making.
- Then listen to the statement. Decide what the speaker is doing.
- Listen again and choose the correct response (a, b or c).

Important! Make sure the other options don't fit the statement.

1 Read the responses. What situation is the person in? What kind of statement is the other person making: a formal introduction, an informal greeting, or saying goodbye?

a See you later.
b How do you do, Mr Smith?
c Hi, Jack. How are you?

2 ⊙*1.11* Listen. What kind of statement do you hear?

3 ⊙*1.11* Listen again and choose the correct response (a, b or c) from Exercise 1.

4 What responses can you give to these statements?

a How do you do?
b Nice to meet you, Mr Brown.
c This is my friend, Lee.

CHECK IT!

5 ⊙*1.12* You will hear four short statements twice. Match each statement with the correct response (a, b or c).

1 a Nice to meet you.
  b See you later!
  c Hi, Erin. How are you?

2 a Bye. See you later.
  b I'm fine. And you?
  c Pleased to meet you.

3 a Hi. I'm fine. And you?
  b Hello, Mr Taggart.
  c How do you do?

4 a Nice to meet you too.
  b See you later!
  c Hello. How are you?

Writing Insights

Spelling: plural nouns and *ing* form

1 Write the plural forms of these nouns. Look at the *Spelling* section in the Writing Bank.

1 flat ....

2 house ....

3 study ....

4 hero ....

5 fish ....

6 class ....

7 match ....

8 box ....

9 life ....

10 woman ....

2 Complete the sentences with the *ing* form of the verbs in brackets. Look at the *Spelling* section in the *Writing bank*.

1 John's .... (study) at university.

2 Mum's .... (call) me for dinner.

3 He's .... (practise) the violin.

4 They're .... (make) biscuits.

5 She's .... (sit) on the sofa.

6 I'm .... (write) a letter.

Punctuation: full stops and question marks

3 Re-write the sentences using capital letters, full stops (.) and question marks (?) where necessary.

1 my brother is good at science

2 do you like chocolate cake

3 can i borrow your book

4 i always do my homework in the evening

5 where do you live

4 Re-write the paragraph in your notebook with capital letters and full stops (.). It should have five sentences.

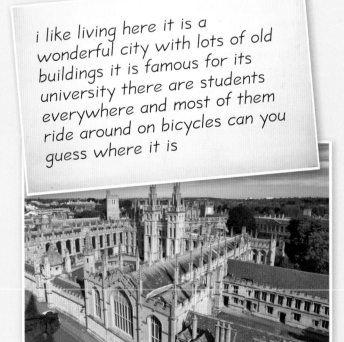

i like living here it is a wonderful city with lots of old buildings it is famous for its university there are students everywhere and most of them ride around on bicycles can you guess where it is

Grammar: word order

5 Write the words in the correct order to make sentences and questions. Don't forget to use capital letters and full stops where needed.

1 cereal / ate / for / Sam / breakfast /

2 geography / Gina / like / doesn't /

3 after / do / do / sport / you / school / ? /

4 well / cousin / swim / your / can / ? /

5 at / teachers / my / strict / are / school / the /

Writing practice: joining sentences

6 Join the sentences with *and* or *but*. Write the sentences in your notebook. Make any other necessary changes.

1 Our flat has a large kitchen. It's got a large living room.

2 We haven't got a garden. We've got a big balcony.

3 There are three bedrooms. There is a bathroom.

4 We're on the fourth floor. We haven't got a nice view.

5 My favourite room is my bedroom. The living room, too.

7 Make notes in your notebook for an email to a new pen friend.

Name: ....

Family: ....

....

....

Where you live: ....

Your school: ....

....

....

Your hobbies: ....

....

....

Favourite subjects: ....

....

....

8 Use three or four of the ideas in your notes and write your email in your notebook. Join your ideas together with *and* or *but*. Check your punctuation.

9 Work in pairs. Read your partner's email. What do you like about it?

Spelling: plural nouns

noun + s

To create the plural form, you add s to most nouns.

rooms, gardens, shops, toys, friends

However, there are other spelling rules that you need to learn. These depend on the last letter(s) of the noun.

Nouns ending in s, x, ch, sh: add es	bus	→	buses
	fox	→	foxes
	watch	→	watches
	wish	→	wishes
Nouns ending in consonant + y: change y to i and add es	baby	→	babies
	study	→	studies
Note: nouns which have a vowel before the y just add s. Example: toys, boys			
Nouns ending in f or fe: change f to v and add es	knife	→	knives
	life	→	lives
	wife	→	wives
	yourself	→	yourselves
Nouns ending in o: add es	potato	→	potatoes
	hero	→	heroes
	tomato	→	tomatoes
Some common irregular plurals	child		children
	person		people
	man/woman		men/women
	fish		fish
	mouse		mice
	tooth		teeth

Spelling: gerunds

Gerunds are nouns formed from verbs by adding *ing*. Here are some simple spelling rules.

+ing One syllable verbs ending in a vowel, verbs with two or more consonants, and verbs with more than one vowel before a consonant, just add *ing*.	be	→	being
	do	→	doing
	walk	→	walking
	study	→	studying
	eat	→	eating
Double consonant +ing Verbs ending in one vowel + one consonant, double the consonant and add *ing*.	stop + p + ing → stopping		
Verbs ending in one vowel + one consonant and the last syllable is stressed.	begin + n + ing → beginning		
Delete the e and add ing Verbs ending with a consonant +e	decide + ing → deciding		
Note: ed verb endings The same spelling rules apply when you add an *ed* ending to a verb:	walked, decided, stopped		
Exceptions to this rule are verbs ending in y: change y to i	studied		

Punctuation: capital letters and full stops

All sentences begin with a capital letter and end with a full stop. There is a space between the full stop (.) and the beginning of the next sentence. Questions end with a question mark (?) The first person singular 'I' is always a capital letter.

A: *How are you?*

B: *I'm fine. And you?*

Grammar: word order in simple sentences

Statements:

Subject + Verb + Object + Complement

(adjective, adverb, time expression etc.)

Questions:

Verb be (or Auxiliary verb) + Subject + Verb + Object + Complement

When we form a question, the verb and the subject change position:

The students are friendly.   *Misha can sing.*

Are the students friendly?   *Can Misha sing?*

John played football yesterday.

Did John play football yesterday?

The same word order for questions follows after a question word (*What, Where, When*, etc.).

What did John play yesterday?

When did John play football?

Useful expressions: personal emails

Beginning your email:
Say *hello*:
Dear ... , / Hello ... , / Hi Ahmed,

Refer to previous email:
Thank you for your email. It was great to hear from you.
Many thanks for your email.

Express good wishes:
I hope you / your family are well.
I hope your exams went well.

Ending your email:
Give a reason for finishing:
Sorry, I must go now. I still have to do my homework.
I must stop writing now. Mum is calling me for my dinner.

Send hopes and wishes:
Hope to hear from you soon. / Write soon.
Best wishes, / Love, (between girls or family members)

2

Performers and artists

GRAMMAR
Learn about *there was / there were,* the past simple, the past continuous and the present perfect.

SKILLS
Read about the history of hip-hop, musical lives, and artists' lives and work.

Listen to a biography of a musician, and people's opinions of an artist's work.

Write a diary.

COMMUNICATE!
Ask for information on the phone.

VOCABULARY
Learn words for music, musicians, and adjectives to describe music.

Work with adjectives, nouns, and verbs.

Music	
classical	opera
folk	pop
hip-hop	traditional
jazz	

1 Work in pairs. Look at the photo. What is it? What kind of music do you play on this instrument?

2 ⊙ 2.1 Listen to six music clips. What styles of music can you hear? Write the numbers (1–6) next to the names of the styles in the vocabulary box.

3 Work in pairs. Which musical styles are popular in your country? How many artists can you name?

4 Answer the questions for yourself. Then work in pairs and ask your partner. What have you got in common?

1 What kind of music do you listen to?
2 Who are your favourite performers?
3 Did you go to any concerts last year? Which ones?
4 Do you play any instruments? Which ones?

Reading and listening

1 Work in pairs. How much do you know about hip-hop? Compare your answers with another pair.

Hip-hop trivia:
which is the correct answer?

1 Hip-hop artists wear
a) expensive fashions. b) sporty clothes.

2 The DJ plays
a) records. b) CDs.

3 The DJ uses
a) an MP3 player. b) turntables.

4 The singer is called
a) the MC. b) the crew.

CHECK IT!

2 ◉ *2.2* Read and listen to the text. What is it about?

a Hip-hop culture in Africa and Europe

b The most famous hip-hop artists today

c The history of hip-hop music

3 Read the text again. Are the sentences true or false?

1 Traditional storytelling styles came to America from Africa.

2 Hip-hop began in Senegal.

3 The first rappers were Missy Elliot and Timbaland.

4 James McBride was a DJ.

Working with words: nouns ▸ adjectives

4 Look at the examples. Then find another similar adjective in the text.

tradition: *I was looking for a traditional storyteller.*

talent: *There were talented new dancers.*

⟩⟩ *See Working with words, Page 117* ⟩

Hip-hop planet

by James McBride, jazz musician and author

You can find hip-hop everywhere you go. Countries like France, Brazil and even Japan have their own hip-hop culture. But where did this strange speaking–singing style come from? Many centuries ago, in West Africa, traditional storytellers played musical instruments while they were telling stories. When this tradition travelled from West Africa to the USA, it developed into different musical styles. For example, blues, jazz and soul music. These styles all started in poor, African-American areas. And in the 1970s, there were a lot of poor areas in New York. There wasn't any money for music lessons in schools, so kids made their own music. Teenagers Afrika Bambaataa and Kool DJ Herc played their records outside in the streets. Everybody joined in. MCs had rapping competitions. Every week, there were talented new dancers, new DJs and new MCs. Hip-hop culture was born.

I remember the first time I heard hip-hop. It was 1980. I was at a party in New York. There was a young DJ at the party. He was playing records on two turntables. While he was putting a record on, a kid picked up a microphone and began rapping. Some other kids were break-dancing to the music. It was loud and repetitive, and I hated it. I preferred jazz.

During the 1980s, hip-hop became popular all over the USA. Today's successful artists like Missy Elliot and her friend Tim Mosley (Timbaland) heard it on the radio when they were growing up.

The last time I heard hip-hop, I was in Senegal, West Africa. I was writing a book about African-Americans. I was going to interview a traditional storyteller when I met a young hip-hop artist. He told me there are hundreds of rap groups in Africa today. We live on a hip-hop planet.

Grammar: *there was / there were*

5 **Complete the sentences from the text.**

1 There _____ a young DJ at the party.

2 There _____ a lot of poor areas in New York.

3 There _____ any money for music lessons in schools.

 See Grammar GPS, Page 125

6 **Read the first sentence. Complete the second sentence so that it gives the same information.**

1 a A lot of people were at the party.
  b There _____ a lot of people at the party.

2 a CDs didn't exist in the 1970s.
  b There _____ any CDs in the 1970s.

3 a The band didn't have a singer.
  b There _____ a singer with the band.

4 a The radio played some great music.
  b There _____ some great music on the radio.

Grammar: past simple and past continuous

7 **Underline the past simple verbs and ⟨circle⟩ the past continuous verbs in the text.**

8 **Write *past simple* or *past continuous* for each use.**

1 an activity in progress at a specific time

_____

2 a completed action at a specific time

_____

3 a sequence of completed actions

_____

 See Grammar GPS, Page 125

9 **Complete the sentences from the text with *when, while* or *during*.**

1 _____ this tradition travelled from West Africa to the USA, it developed into different musical styles.

2 _____ he was putting a record on, a kid picked up a microphone and began rapping.

3 _____ the 1980s, hip-hop became popular all over America.

4 I was going to interview a traditional storyteller _____ I met a young hip-hop artist.

 See Grammar GPS, Page 125

10 **Complete the text with the past simple or past continuous form of the verbs.**

Missy Elliot and Tim Mosley (**1** grow up) *grew up* in the same town. Missy Elliot (**2** start) _____ her band, Sista, in 1990. She (**3** sing) _____ with her band when a New York record producer (**4** hear) _____ her. She (**5** move) _____ to New York. Tim Mosley (**6** go) _____ with her and he (**7** change) _____ his name to Timbaland. While she (**8** live) _____ in New York, Missy Elliot (**9** write) _____ songs for other hip-hop artists. Timbaland and Missy Elliot both (**10** become) _____ international stars in the 1990s.

Speaking

11 **Match the comments (1–4) with the pictures (a–d).**

1 'I think it's sad.'
2 'I can't stand it. It's too loud.'
3 'I like it. It's catchy.'
4 'I don't mind it. It's a bit boring.'

12 **Work in pairs. What do you think of the different styles of music on page 17? Use the adjectives in the box.**

awful	boring	catchy	exciting
great	happy	loud	relaxing	repetitive
sad	strange		

If you have time

How many adjectives do you know to describe these things? Write at least five adjectives for each thing. Then write adjectives with the opposite meaning.

performers	sports	people
places you go	food	

Vocabulary: musicians and instruments

1 Look at the words for musicians. Which ones play instruments? Which instruments do they play?

> artist   composer   conductor   drummer
> guitarist   keyboard player   pianist
> singer   violinist   accordionist   'oud player

2 Work in pairs. Compare your answers to Exercise 1. How many more instruments can you name?

Working with words: nouns and verbs ▶ nouns

3 Look at the examples. Which nouns in Exercise 1 have got a similar form?

guitar: *I want to be a guitarist.*
drum: *My uncle is a drummer.*

➤➤➤ *See Working with words, Page 117* ➤

Reading and listening

STUDY SKILLS

4 Read the text quickly. How many words for musicians and instruments can you find?

5 🔊 **2.3** Read and listen to the text. Find the names of five people. What have they got in common?

6 Read the text again. Complete the sentences with the correct names.

1 _____ plays in a group.
2 _____ doesn't go to an ordinary school.
3 _____ plays two instruments.
4 _____ and _____ write and perform music.

Speaking

7 Work in groups of four. Read the last paragraph of the text again. Give your opinions.

A: I think Lara's life has been better than mine because she's famous.

B: I don't agree. She spends all her time practising.

Musical lives

What does it feel like to give a concert performance at the age of seven? Or to be famous when you are ten? These were the experiences of classical musicians such as Chopin and Mozart. They spent all of their time practising the piano or writing music. So what about some of today's talented young musicians? Has music dominated their lives?

'Oud player Mohamed Abozekry was born in Cairo. He graduated from the Arabic 'Oud House when he was only 15 and became the youngest 'oud teacher in the Middle East. In 2009, he won the International 'Oud Competition in Damascus. Mohamed has performed around the world with his quartet Heejaz. He spends a lot of his time composing music for the group.

Lara Melda had her first piano lesson when she was 6. She was born in London, but her parents are Turkish. She won the BBC Young Musician 2010 competition and has given many concerts in Britain and Turkey. Lara practises the piano for five or six hours a day, as well as playing the viola and attending the Purcell School, for young musicians, in London.

Composer, conductor and pianist Alex Prior has had a similar life. He's only 17, but he's written over 40 pieces of music. When he was growing up, he spent most of his time on his music and did school lessons at home for a year. He then entered the St Petersburg State Conservatory of Music, in Russia.

These three young people have become very successful. But have their lives been better or worse than ordinary kids' lives? What do you think?

Grammar: present perfect

8 Complete the sentences from the text.

1 Mohamed _____ around the world with his quartet, Heejaz.

2 These three young people _____ very successful.

3 But _____ their lives _____ better or worse than ordinary kids' lives?

Note that the present perfect form – the past participle – of some verbs is irregular: *begin – begun*. Note also that some verbs have two present perfect forms: *learn – learned/learnt*.

9 <u>Underline</u> three more present perfect verbs in the text. Read the rule below and choose the correct option.

We use the present perfect when we *know / don't know* the date of the event.

 See Grammar GPS, Page 125

10 Complete the sentences with the present perfect form of the verbs.

Cheb Khaled is a singer-songwriter from Algeria. He (**1** write) _____ many internationally popular songs and (**2** sell) _____ over 46 million albums. He (**3** work) _____ with hip-hop artists and symphony orchestras and (**4** perform) _____ live at music and arts festivals around the world. He (**5** win) _____ over 15 music awards. He (**6** not/be) _____ as big in the UK or the USA, but he (**7** attract) _____ millions of fans all over Europe, Canada, the Middle East, Asia and Brazil.

Listening

11  **2.4** Listen to the biography of the violinist Vanessa-Mae. Tick the words you hear.

| London | talent | performed | pop |
| classical | awards | festival | |

CHECK IT!

12 **2.4** Listen again and complete the notes.

1 Vanessa-Mae was born in _____ .

2 She plays the _____ and the _____ .

3 She recorded Beethoven and Tchaikovsky when she was _____ .

4 She has recorded with _____ and _____ .

5 She has sold more than _____ albums.

Speaking

13 Work in pairs. Do you think Vanessa-Mae is unusual? Why? / Why not?

14 Make notes about a musician or singer. Then work in pairs. Take turns to describe the person, and to ask and answer questions. Can you guess your partner's person?

A: *... and he's won a lot of MTV awards.*

B: *Has he been in any films?*

STUDY SKILLS

Topic words

1 Look and listen for words that are connected to the same topic.

2 Learn the words by writing them in groups: *orchestral instruments – violin, piano, ...*

3 Use your own categories to organise words: *music I like: jazz, hip-hop, folk songs, ...*

Reading and listening

1 ⊙ **2.5** Read and listen to the dialogue. What does Lee ask for information about?

a pop concerts
b musical shows
c art exhibitions

Salesman: Hello, West End Box Office. How can I help you?

Lee: Hello. I'm phoning about tickets for this Saturday.

Salesman: Which show would you like to see?

Lee: Have you got tickets for *Abba, the Musical*?

Salesman: Sorry. There aren't any tickets left for *Abba*.

Lee: What about *Les Miserables*? Or *Stomp*?

Salesman: I'm afraid we've only got tickets for the afternoon performance of *Stomp*.

Lee: Oh, right. What time does the show start?

Salesman: It starts at four o'clock.

Lee: OK. How much do the tickets cost?

Salesman: They're fifty pounds each.

Lee: Fifty pounds! Can you hold on a moment, please?

Reem: That's OK for me. My mum's buying the ticket for my birthday.

Lee: Yes, but what about Lauren and Jack?

Reem: We can phone them and ask.

Lee: Hello? Sorry to keep you waiting. Can I phone back later?

Salesman: Yes, of course.

Lee: Great. Thanks for your help.

Salesman: You're welcome. Goodbye.

Lee: Goodbye.

2 Read the dialogue again. Why doesn't Lee buy any tickets?

a There aren't any tickets left.
b He hasn't got any money.
c He wants to talk to Lauren and Jack first.

3 Read the dialogue again. Put the *Useful expressions* in the correct order (1–10) and decide who says them. Write L for Lee or S for the salesman.

Useful expressions

.... I'm phoning about (tickets for this Saturday).
.... Sorry. There aren't any tickets left (for *Abba*).
.... How much do (the tickets) cost?
.... You're welcome.
.... How can I help you?
.... Can you hold on a moment, please?
.... What time does (the show start)?
.... Can I phone back later?
.... Thanks for your help.
.... I'm afraid we've only got tickets for (the afternoon performance of *Stomp*).

4 ⊙ **2.6** Listen and repeat the *Useful expressions*. Focus on your intonation.

5 ◉**2.7** Listen to the conversation and complete the information.

Time: ....

Day: ....

Price: ....

6 Complete the dialogue. Use the *Useful expressions* to help you.

Salesman: Hello. Box Office.
(1) .... ?

Lee: (2) ....
tickets for *Stomp* this Saturday.

Salesman: I'm afraid (3) ....
.... for Saturday afternoon.

Lee: Oh, OK. I need to talk to my friends first. (4) ....
.... ?

Salesman: Yes, of course.

Lee: (5) ....

Salesman: You're welcome.

Speaking

7 Work in pairs. Take turns asking for and giving information about these events.

A: Decide which event you want to go to. Phone the box office for information about days, times and prices.

B: You work in the box office. You haven't got many tickets left. For each event, choose only one day when there are tickets left.

Pronunciation: the sounds /t/ and /d/ before /j/

8 ◉**2.8** Listen. Which sound joins the underlined words? (Circle) /tʃ/ or /dʒ/.

A: *Have you got your ticket yet?*   /tʃ/   /dʒ/

B: *Yes, it arrived yesterday.*   /tʃ/   /dʒ/

9 ◉**2.9** Listen and repeat the sentences.

1 When di<u>d y</u>ou last go to a concert?
2 Vanessa-Mae sold millions of albums las<u>t y</u>ear.
3 I like classical music, bu<u>t y</u>ou don't.
4 The music festival ende<u>d y</u>esterday.

Writing: a diary

1 Read Reem's diary entry. Answer the questions.

1 Where did Reem go?
2 Who did she go with?
3 Which places did she visit?
4 What were her opinions?
5 What did she do after the show?

2 Underline *after, after that, before, during, first, in the end* and *then* in the diary entry.

3 Choose the correct option or options.

I went shopping today. (1) *First, / During / Before* I bought some clothes. (2) *After / After that, / Then,* I had lunch in a burger bar. I wanted a salad, but they were sold out. (3) *Before / First, / In the end,* I had a cheeseburger. (4) *After that, / Before / After* lunch, I went to the bookshop. (5) *Then, / After that, / During* I caught the bus home.

4 Write a diary entry about a day in your recent past. Use the questions in Exercise 1 to help you plan your paragraph. Remember to include words from Exercise 2.

October

10 *Saturday*

I had a great time in London today! I got up really early and met Lauren, Jack and Lee at the station. Before I left the house, my dad gave me £50 spending money! We caught the train to London and arrived at ten o'clock. First, we visited the Modern Art Museum. The art was strange, but some of it was amazing! Then, we looked round the museum shop. After that, we were really hungry, so we bought some sandwiches and ate them in the park.
In the afternoon, we went to the theatre to see Stomp! It was absolutely fantastic. During the show, the audience joined in, clapping their hands. After the show, we were thirsty and wanted to have a drink in the theatre café. It was too busy, so we went to a café across the road, but there weren't any free tables. In the end, we bought some cans of lemonade from a machine and then caught the train back home.

Reading

1 Work in pairs. Look at the photos of pieces of artwork. What is your opinion of them?

2 ⊙2.10 Listen and read the text. Match the photos (A–C) with the artists (1–3).

3 Read the text again. Complete the sentences with the names of the artists; *Kapoor*, *Kngwarreye* or *Labbauf*.

1 _____ painted pictures of places.
2 _____ works with other people.
3 You don't need to go to an exhibition to see work by _____ .
4 _____ is influenced by other styles of art.
5 _____ 's art is now very expensive.

4 Find words in the text for these things.

1 places to see art
2 types of artwork
3 adjectives to describe size

Listening

5 ⊙2.11 Listen to three people's opinions of one of the artists. Which artist are they talking about?

a Anish Kapoor
b Emily Kame Kngwarreye
c Farsad Labbauf

Culture

Art produced in the last fifty years is known as contemporary art. Read about the work of three famous contemporary artists.

1 Anish Kapoor was born in India in 1954. He moved to London in the 1970s to study art. He is now a famous sculptor, with exhibitions all over the world. His enormous sculptures are made from solid stone or polished steel. Kapoor works with architects and engineers to build giant structures in public places. His most famous public sculptures are *Sky Mirror*, in New York, and *Cloud Gate*, in Chicago. These massive, reflective shapes took two years to complete. He also built *Temenos*, a vast sculpture that looks like a butterfly net, located in Middlesbrough, UK. It is the biggest public artwork in the world.

A

B

Joseph – (smile)

2 Aboriginal artist **Emily Kame Kngwarreye** was 80 when she started painting. Before she died in 1996, she produced more than 3000 acrylic paintings. She used traditional aboriginal techniques such as dots, stripes and lines. During her lifetime she had exhibitions in museums and galleries around the world. Her most famous work, *Earth's Creation*, is a huge, colourful landscape measuring 6.3m × 2.7m. Emily Kngwarreye's paintings represent her ancestors as well as the plants, animals, colours and landscapes of the Simpson Desert in central Australia. *Earth's Creation* has become Australia's most important painting. In 2007, it sold for more than a million dollars.

C

6 ⊙ *2.11* **Listen again. Write the number of the speaker (1, 2 or 3) next to the summarising sentences.**

1 I don't mind his work. It's quite good. ☐

2 I think his work is exciting. ☐

3 I think his art is a waste of money. ☐

4 He's not an artist at all! ☐

5 His ideas are original. ☐

Write about your favourite artist or performer. Write about their life and give your opinion of their work.

③

Farsad Labbauf was born in Iran in 1965. He now lives in New York and paints huge portraits of people from his country. He is inspired by traditional Persian arts, including calligraphy and tapestry. His paintings are made up of hundreds of individual lines and shapes. From a distance, the portraits look very realistic. Labbauf is famous in Iran and the United States. He has had exhibitions in the Middle East, Europe and the USA. In 2009, the Saatchi Gallery in London included his work in the exhibition *New Art from the Middle East.*

Art and English:
Vincent van Gogh

1 How much do you know about Vincent van Gogh and his work? Answer the questions.

1 What are two of van Gogh's most famous paintings?

2 Why didn't people buy his art when he was alive?

3 Why was Theo so important to van Gogh?

2 Read the text and check your answers.

Vincent van Gogh (1853–1890)

Vincent van Gogh was born in Holland in 1853. He started painting when he was 27 years old. He started classes at famous art schools, but he wasn't happy there and he didn't stay long. In 1886, he lived with his brother, Theo, in Paris and painted scenes of the city. In 1888, he moved to the south of France, where he painted many of his most famous pictures, including *Vase with 12 Sunflowers* and *The Starry Night.*

During his life, van Gogh had periods of extreme depression. At other times, he was happy and optimistic, and produced hundreds of paintings. Van Gogh died in 1890.

Van Gogh's style of painting was new and controversial, and nobody wanted to buy his work. During his life, van Gogh only sold one painting, in 1888.

Vincent and Theo

Vincent's brother, Theo, was an art dealer. The two brothers often wrote to each other. Theo encouraged Vincent to continue painting and often sent him money to help him. Vincent's work became very popular in the late 20th century and his pictures now sell for record-breaking prices. Today he is one of the most important and popular artists in Western art.

Self Portrait by van Gogh

Reading

HOW TO...

identify the main idea of a text

- Read the whole text quickly. Decide what you think the main topic of the text is.
- Read the text again and look for words that are connected to that topic. This helps you check your decision.
- Look at the options in the question. Which one matches your decision the best?
- Read the text again. Check the alternative options and make sure.

Important! You need to read the whole text to find the main idea.

1 Read the text quickly. What do you think the main topic of the text is?

Last year my family moved to Edinburgh. I didn't want to go. I hated my new school at first, but I made lots of new friends and now I like it. When I started at the new school, it was difficult to understand my teachers' Scottish accent. Now, when I phone my grandparents in London, they say I'm starting to get a Scottish accent!

2 Underline words that you think are connected to your answer to Exercise 1.

3 Which option (a–c) matches your answer to Exercise 1?

- **a** Living in Scotland
- **b** Moving to a new place
- **c** Living with my family

CHECK IT!

4 Read the text and choose the correct option (a–c).

I started to be interested in music when I was about ten years old. I was learning the piano at school and I enjoyed the lessons very much. Then I went to music classes with a private teacher. I learnt the violin and the trumpet, but I was best at the piano. While I was practising one day, I realised that I enjoyed making up songs more than playing other people's music. I was about 12 years old. I often wrote music during my music lessons at school because I wasn't interested in other types of music!

What is the text about?

- **a** The writer's ambitions as a musician.
- **b** The writer's experiences of music as a student.
- **c** The writer's experience as a professional musician.

Listening

HOW TO...

identify detailed information

- Read the questions carefully before you listen. Try to predict the information you will hear.
- For gap-fill questions, decide what type of information goes into the gap.
- For true or false statements, underline the key words in the statements.

Important! Answer the questions the first time you listen. Check your answers the second time.

1 Look at the form. Match the information (a–d) with the gaps (1–4).

- **a** Richardson
- **b** Saturday
- **c** afternoon
- **d** six

The Prince's Theatre
Booking form

Day:	(1) ....
Performance:	(2) ....
Number of tickets:	(3) ....
Name:	(4) ....

2 🔘 *2.12* Listen and check your answers.

3 Look at this task. What type of information is missing in each gap? Choose the correct option.

Listen to the information about a singer and complete the information.
1 He was born in ....
  a a name   **b** a date
2 He sings with ....
  a a place   **b** the name of a band
3 He plays ....
  a an instrument   **b** a number
4 His band has sold .... albums.
  a a place   **b** a number

4 🔘 *2.13* Listen and check your answers.

CHECK IT!

5 🔘 *2.14* Listen to the message and complete the missing information.

Opening hours: 10 a.m. to (1) ....
Monday to Friday
Tickets for (2) .... evening
performances are sold out.
Tickets cost: £35, (3) .... and £65.
There are discounts for (4) ....

Writing Insights

Punctuation: sentence punctuation

1 Punctuate the paragraph with commas (,) and full stops (.) to make three sentences. Remember to use a capital letters after a full stop!

I've joined the drama club because I love singing playing and acting last year I played the violin but I didn't like it it was boring the teacher was very strict and the strings hurt my fingers

Punctuation: joining ideas

2 Join the ideas together to make two sentences.

Naila didn't enjoy the concert.
The room was too hot.
She lost her bag.
The band was terrible.

Grammar: adjectives in a sentence

3 Cross out the extra word.

1 A pair of green socks green.
2 That's fantastic a fantastic piece of music.
3 The journey was a long and boring.
4 Do you like traditional and Arabic music?
5 He's not a not clever man.

4 Choose the best group of adjectives (a–e) and put them in the correct order to complete the descriptions (1–5). Look at the *Grammar* section in the *Writing bank*.

a plastic Chinese cheap   **d** narrow busy short
b old dirty London red   **e** Italian new leather
c big beautiful yellow   brown

1 Some _____ flowers.
2 A _____ street.
3 A _____ toy.
4 A pair of _____ boots.
5 A _____ bus.

Writing practice: narratives

5 Write the correct punctuation in this paragraph to make four sentences. Remember to use a capital letter after a full stop!

on sunday afternoon we went to the cinema first we bought our tickets then I bought some popcorn before the film started we had a coffee at the café and after that we went in and found our seats

Writing practice: narratives

6 Complete the paragraphs with sequencers from the box. Use the *Writing bank* to help you. There is one extra word in each box.

| after | first | last | Saturday | then |

(1) On _____ , my father and I went to see a football match. It was a very long day.
(2) _____ , we got up at seven o'clock and had breakfast. **(3)** _____ , my dad drove us to the bus station. We caught the bus to Liverpool and arrived six hours later.

| after | after that | before | in the end |

(4) _____ we arrived in Liverpool, we bought some sandwiches and ate them in a café. **(5)** _____ , we walked to the stadium and watched the match. When the match finished, we went back to the bus station. The next bus left at midnight!
(6) _____ , we didn't get home until five in the morning!

7 In your notebook, put the extract from the diary entry in the correct order. Join the ideas together with sequencers and time expressions. Begin your paragraph, '*Last Monday…*'

September

12th *Monday*

The teacher told us to be quiet.
The teacher introduced her to the class.
We started talking.
We didn't speak to each other again until lunchtime.
A new girl started school today.
She sat down next to me.

8 Think of an interesting day or experience you had recently. Write notes about what happened. Use the questions to help you.

Where were you?   What happened first?
What did you do?   What happened next?
Who were you with?   How did it end?

9 Now write a story or a diary entry in your notebook. Use your notes from Exercise 8 and add time expressions and sequencers from Exercise 6.

10 Check your writing. Have you joined your ideas together in a logical order? Have you used sequencers and time expressions? Check your spelling and punctuation.

Punctuation: use of commas to join ideas

We use commas to join three or more ideas to give more information about a topic.

The last two ideas are joined by *and* with no comma.

idea 1   **idea 2**

I saw a comedy on TV last night. The acting was brilliant,

idea 3

the dialogue was wonderful, and it was really funny.

Grammar: position of adjectives

Position of adjectives in noun phrases

This is our new school.

Adjectives that describe a noun are placed before the noun.

Position of adjectives with link verbs

Adjectives that are used to complement a verb are placed after the verb. These verbs are called link verbs. Common link verbs are: *be, become, look, seem* and *feel*. Two adjectives are joined with *and*.

The school is new and modern.

If we use more than two adjectives, we put a comma between them and write *and* before the last adjective. There is no comma before or after *and*.

We felt hot, tired, hungry and thirsty.

What's the difference?

If you remove the adjectives from a noun phrase, it still makes sense. If you remove the adjectives from the link verb phrase, it does not make sense.

I saw a ~~large~~, ~~grey~~ horse in the stable.

I feel ~~sad~~ and ~~lonely~~.

Noun phrases with more than one adjective

When two or more adjectives before a noun, they follow a specific order:

opinion adjectives + **fact** adjectives

A beautiful, Chinese, red, silk dress.

Order of adjectives

Fact adjectives

Fact adjectives follow this order:

size + age + shape + colour + origin + material

A large, square, wooden desk.

Two young, grey, Burmese cats.

When there are two 'size' adjectives, length comes before width.

A long, wide river.

Writing practice: sequencers and time expressions

Sequencers

Common sequencers include:

first   before (leaving the party)   after (the show)
after that   then   in the end

Note: *before* and *after* are followed by a noun or gerund (verb *+ing*).

Sequencers are used at the beginning of a sentence or in the middle of a sentence.

They are always placed before a comma or between commas:

After leaving work, I went shopping. First, I bought a pair of shoes and, after that, I bought some new jeans.

Time expressions

These are used at the beginning (followed by a comma) or at the end of a sentence.

at the weekend
in the morning / afternoon / evening
on Monday (and other days of the week)
last Tuesday
last month / year / June (and other months)
yesterday
yesterday afternoon

My grandmother came to stay at the weekend.

At the weekend, my grandmother came to stay.

We had a lot of exams last month.

Last month, we had a lot of exams.

Useful expressions: narratives and diary entries

Begin with something that will get the reader's attention.

I had a really wonderful time today! We got up early and went to the beach.

(**Not:** *Today, we got up early and went to the beach.*)

End with a conclusion or something about how you felt.

We all arrived back safe and sound.

At the end of the day, I felt tired but very happy!

It was one of the best/worst/most frightening experiences of my life!

Grammar consolidation
Comparing → See Grammar GPS, Page 125

Comparing with adjectives

1 Look at the pictures and complete the sentences.

Ben's school   Dan's school

1 Dan's school is _____ than Ben's school. (big)

2 Dan's school is _____ than Ben's school. (noisy)

3 Ben's school is more _____ than Dan's school. (traditional)

4 Ben's school is less _____ than Dan's school. (modern)

5 Dan thinks his school is _____ than Ben's school. (good)

 We can use *isn't as* + adjective + *as* instead of *less* + adjective + *than*.

2 Look at the example and complete the sentences.

▶ *Ben's school isn't as big as Dan's school.*

1 Ben's school _____ Dan's school. (noisy)

2 Ben's school _____ Dan's school. (modern)

3 Dan's school _____ Ben's school. (traditional)

4 Ben's school _____ Dan's school. (good)

3 Read the first sentence. Complete the second sentence so that it gives the same information.

1 My teachers are more serious than Ben's teachers. Ben's teachers _____

2 My teachers aren't as friendly as Ben's teachers. Ben's teachers _____

3 Ben's school is older than my school. My school is _____

4 Ben's teachers are less strict than my teachers. My teachers _____

4 Which two sentences mean the same thing?

a My school is the same as Ben's school.

b My school isn't the same as Ben's school.

c My school is different from Ben's school.

Comparing with nouns

We can also compare quantities of things with *there is/are* + as *much/many.*

5 Look at the example and complete the sentences with *as much as* or *as many as.*

▶ *In Ben's school, there aren't as many students as in Dan's school.*

1 In Ben's school, there aren't _____ teachers _____ in Dan's school.

2 In Ben's school, there aren't _____ rules _____ in Dan's school.

3 In Ben's school, there isn't _____ discipline _____ in Dan's school.

4 In Ben's school, they don't give _____ homework _____ in Dan's school.

6 Look at the example. Then rewrite the sentences in Exercise 5.

▶ *In Dan's school, there are more students than in Ben's school.*

1 In Dan's school, _____

2 In Dan's school, _____

3 In Dan's school, _____

4 In Dan's school, _____

7 Complete the sentences with *as, than* or *from.*

1 London is different _____ my town.

2 My house is the same _____ your house.

3 Classical music is more boring _____ pop music.

4 Hip-hop isn't as relaxing _____ classical music.

5 There aren't as many musicians in the UK _____ in the USA.

6 I don't listen to as much music _____ my brother.

7 Pop songs are catchier _____ traditional music.

8 Guitar music is different _____ violin music.

Vocabulary

1 Write the places.

1 You sleep here. b_____
2 You do experiments here. l_____
3 You cook food here. k_____
4 Flowers grow here. g_____
5 You eat school lunch here. c_____

1 mark per item: .../5 marks

2 Write the school subjects.

1 physics, biology and c_____ = science
2 French and Italian = l_____
3 p_____ and drawing = art
4 cooking = f_____ t_____
5 geography and h_____ = social sciences

1 mark per item: .../5 marks

3 Complete the sentences with adjectives.

1 My sister does nothing. She's l_____ .
2 My dad is s_____ . He has lots of rules.
3 We laugh because the teacher is f_____ .
4 Everyone is singing that song. It's very c_____ .
5 This music is s_____ . It makes me cry.

1 mark per item: .../5 marks

4 Write the instruments.

1 _____
2 _____
3 _____
4 _____
5 _____

1 mark per item: .../5 marks

5 Complete the sentences.

1 I never like waiting. I'm _____ .
2 I _____ a mistake in my test yesterday.
3 I _____ my homework in my room.
4 Everybody knows this painter. She's very _____ .
5 My friend won first place in a _____ .

1 mark per item: .../5 marks

Grammar

6 Complete the sentences with the present simple or present continuous form of these verbs.

| live   need   play   prefer   want |

1 I _____ pop to traditional music.
2 _____ you _____ some pasta?
3 I _____ a calculator to do this maths.
4 'Where's Jack?' 'He _____ rugby.'
5 My best friend _____ next door to me.

1 mark per item: .../5 marks

7 Complete the paragraph with the present simple or present continuous form of the verbs.

I (**1** learn) _____ the electric guitar this year. My cousin (**2** teach) _____ me. I (**3** practise) _____ in the evenings. My parents (**4** watch) _____ the TV. They (**5** not / like) _____ the noise I make!

1 mark per item: .../5 marks

8 Write affirmative or negative sentences and questions with *there was / there were*.

1 _____ a lot of people in the audience.
2 _____ a concert last night?
3 _____ any tickets for the show.
4 _____ any hip-hop artists in the 1970s?
5 _____ a film on TV last night.

1 mark per item: .../5 marks

9 Complete the paragraph with the past simple or past continuous form of the verbs.

Last week my friend and I (**1** go) _____ to a fantastic concert. After the show, while we (**2** leave) _____ the theatre, we (**3** see) _____ the singer. We (**4** take) _____ his photo while he (**5** get into) _____ his car.

1 mark per item: .../5 marks

10 Complete the sentences.

1 Are you good _____ maths?
2 I fell asleep _____ the film.
3 Geography is easier _____ physics.
4 Mohamed Abozekry was 15 _____ he became an 'oud teacher.
5 Pop music isn't as interesting _____ jazz.

1 mark per item: .../5 marks

Communicate

11 **Complete the dialogue with the expressions.**

> You're welcome.
> How much do they cost?
> I'm phoning about …
> How can I help you?
> Thanks for your help.

Salesman: Hello. City Hall. **(1)** ....

....

Reem: **(2)** ....
tickets for *Chicago*.

Salesman: Yes?

Reem: **(3)** ....

Salesman: We've got some tickets for Friday at £25.

Reem: That's great. **(4)** ....

....

Salesman: **(5)** ....

2 marks per item: …/10 marks

12 **Match the statements (1–5) with the responses (a–e).**

1 Hi, Ben. How are you?

2 How do you do, Mr Brown?

3 Let me introduce my geography teacher, Mrs Short.

4 See you later.

5 This is my friend, Ben.

a How do you do, Emma? Call me Bryan.

b I'm fine. And you?

c Nice to meet you, Ben.

d OK, bye.

e Pleased to meet you.

2 marks per item: …/10 marks

13 **Is the underlined word stressed (S) or unstressed (U)?**

1 Jack's brilliant <u>at</u> maths. ....

2 We had a good time in <u>London</u>. ....

3 Pleased <u>to</u> meet you. ....

4 How do you <u>do</u>? ....

5 Do you want a game <u>of</u> tennis? ....

2 marks per item: …/10 marks

14 **Complete the sentences with these words. Use one word twice.**

> and   because   but   so

1 My maths teacher is serious, ... he isn't strict.

2 On Saturday mornings I meet my friends .... we go shopping.

3 We lost the match, ... everyone's unhappy.

4 We didn't buy tickets .... they were too expensive.

5 I studied a lot, ... I didn't pass my exam.

2 marks per item: …/10 marks

15 **Complete the story with these words.**

> after   any   because   first   for   in the end
> next   so   then   while

I spent a lot of time in town yesterday!
(1) .... , I met Emma and we did some shopping. Emma wanted to buy some jeans, **(2)** .... we went to a clothes shop. **(3)** .... we were paying for the jeans, we saw Amy. She was waiting for Ben. We talked to Amy for a few minutes. **(4)** .... we all went for something to eat. While we were eating, Ben arrived. I gave him some of my pasta **(5)** .... I wasn't very hungry. **(6)** .... lunch, we went shopping again! Ben wanted to buy a Celine Dion CD **(7)** .... his mum. It's her birthday **(8)** .... week. We tried all the shops, but there weren't **(9)** .... Celine Dion CDs! **(10)** .... , he bought a scarf.

1 mark per item: …/10 marks

Total: …/100

I can...			
Tick (✔) what you can do.			
	★★★★★	★★★	★
I can make informal greetings and introductions.			
I can make formal greetings and introductions.			
I can ask for information on the phone.			

True story:
Looking for adventure

1 Read the text and answer the questions.

1 What was Wilfred Thesiger's ambition when he was a child?

2 Why did he stay with the Bedouin for five years?

3 Where did he write many of his books?

4 When did his ambition come true?

2 Read the text again. Find nouns and adjectives made from these words.

> tribe   adventure   discover   hungry   thirsty   courage

3 Use the fact file to write questions. Then work with a partner and test your memory. Ask and answer the questions.

▶ *How many photographs did Thesiger take?*

4 Work in groups. What do you think life was like for Thesiger when he was in the desert?

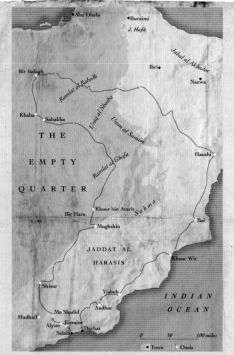

The Empty Quarter: Thesiger's first crossing

Fact file

38,000	the photographs he took
11	the awards he received from universities and societies
11	the books he wrote
3	the awards he received from Queen Elizabeth II
2,400	the distance he travelled across the Empty Quarter (km)
402,330	the size of the Empty Quarter (square kms)
3,050	the height of sand dunes in the Arabian Desert (metres)

'The two of us will go with you wherever you want.' *Salim bin Kabina*

Thesiger's adventures in Africa were certainly interesting, but he wanted to be like the great British Victorian explorers. He wanted to travel across undiscovered lands and learn about other cultures. His big ambition was to go to the southern Arabian Desert, known as The Empty Quarter. In 1946, he joined the nomadic Bedu tribes. He stayed with them for five years and crossed the Empty Quarter twice. His time there was hard. He suffered from terrible hunger and thirst. He often had nothing to eat for several days and very little water to drink. He was also afraid that some of the tribesmen wanted to kill him. But his years in the army, and his experiences in Africa, had taught him how to survive. Thesiger loved the Bedu. They were courageous, loyal and generous. They loved and respected him too, and called him Mubarak Bin London. Thesiger described his time with them as the best years of his life.

Wilfred Thesiger was British, but he grew up among the native people of Ethiopia. As a child he experienced the excitement of tribal wars and lion hunting. When he was 14, he knew that he wanted to be a famous adventurer and discover unknown places. After studying at Eton and Oxford University, Wilfred Thesiger went back to Africa many times. During the 1930s he went on an expedition to explore the River Awash in Ethiopia. He was also an army officer in the Sudan.

After leaving the Bedu, Thesiger lived among the Marsh Arabs in Iraq for seven years. He trekked across the Hindu Kush mountains and across Morocco. After that, he travelled around Kurdistan, Pakistan, Persia and West Africa. From Ethiopia he journeyed by camel to Lake Turkana, in northern Kenya. For the next 35 years, Thesiger lived and travelled in Kenya, where he wrote most of his books, including two travel books, *Arabian Sands* (1959) and *The Marsh Arabs* (1964).

Your health

GRAMMAR
Learn about the present perfect with *yet*, *already* and *just*; *for* and *since*; and the uses of the present perfect and past simple.

SKILLS
Read about health news, teen problems, and the *Malaria No More* campaign.

Listen to a radio programme about Lance Armstrong, and the *Malaria No More* campaign.

Write an article.

COMMUNICATE!
Agree and disagree.

VOCABULARY
Learn words for health problems, and activities.

Work with noun + noun collocations, and adjective + preposition combinations.

Health problems	
an allergy	hay fever
asthma	a headache
bronchitis	measles
chicken pox	a nosebleed
a cold	a rash
a cough	a sore throat
earache	tonsillitis
flu	toothache

1 Work in pairs. Look at the photo. What do you think it is? Why?

  a a red blood cell

  b the measles virus

  c the chemical structure of aspirin

2 ☉ *3.1* Listen to two conversations and an answerphone message. Write the numbers (1–3) next to the words you hear in the Vocabulary box. What's wrong with the people?

3 Work in pairs. What are the symptoms of these illnesses? Use words from the Vocabulary box and your own ideas.

bronchitis   flu   measles   tonsillitis

4 What are the most common health problems in your class? Write two questions for each prompt. Then ask at least three people.

Have you ever had … ?

Have you ever been off school with … ?

Have you ever been to hospital with … ?

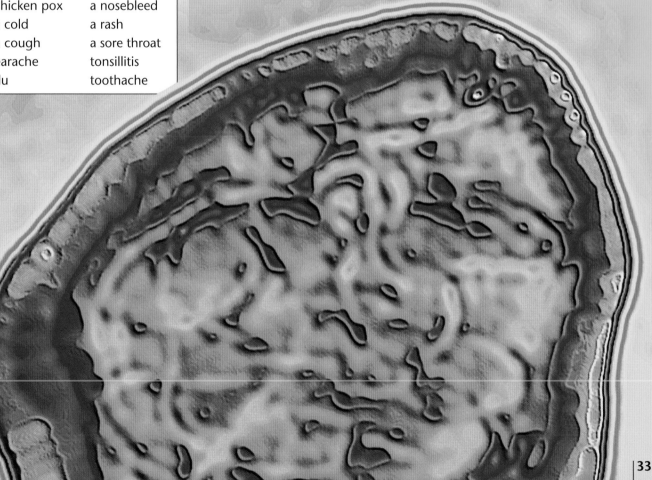

Reading and listening

CHECK IT!

1 Read the news stories quickly. Match the headlines (1–5) with the stories (A–D). There is one extra headline.

1 Honey makes your skin healthy
2 An answer to the flu mystery
3 A new treatment for asthma
4 How snails can be good for your health
5 More tropical illnesses in holidaymakers

2 ○ **3.2** Read and listen to the news stories. Complete the table.

	Illness	Cause	Prevention or treatment
A	flu	....	stay ...., drink lots of liquids, take ....
B	skin infections	bacteria	.... and ....
C	tropical diseases, ...	–	.... and ....
D	epilepsy	–	....

Working with words: noun + noun

3 Look at the examples. Which nouns can go before *ache* to give words for health problems?

flu + virus = flu virus   pain + killer = painkiller

➤➤ *See Working with words, Page 118* ➤

Grammar: present perfect with *yet*, *already* and *just*

4 Complete the sentences from the news stories.

1 But a new study has .... shown that the flu virus prefers the cold, dry air in winter.
2 The hospital has used the new bandages for a week and they have .... had excellent results.
3 Have you had all your vaccinations .... ?
4 Several people have already died from its sting because scientists haven't found a cure ....

➤➤ *See Grammar GPS, Pages 126–127* ➤

A

The Daily News

Have you had flu yet this winter? Why do more people get flu in winter than in summer? This fact has puzzled scientists for many years. But a new study has just shown that the flu virus prefers the cold, dry air in winter. Perhaps this means that the usual advice for treating flu symptoms is correct: stay warm and drink a lot of liquids. And remember: take painkillers, not antibiotics, for viral illnesses!

B

You probably like the taste of honey, but have you ever put it on your skin? A London hospital has just announced a new treatment for cuts, burns and skin infections, using honey bandages. The usual treatment with antibiotics often doesn't work because many bacteria have become resistant to antibiotics. However, honey kills bacteria. The hospital has used the new bandages for a week and they have already had excellent results.

C

Are you travelling abroad for your holidays this year? Have you had all your vaccinations yet? According to doctors, the number of holidaymakers returning home from remote areas with tropical diseases has increased. One doctor said, 'I've seen five people with yellow fever since March. That's very unusual. People should take tablets and get vaccinations when they travel.'

D

Be careful! The poison from this beautiful cone snail is strong enough to kill you. Several people have already died from its sting because scientists haven't found a cure yet. However, doctors have known for a long time that some poisons can be useful. Now, they have developed a painkiller and a medicine for epilepsy from the cone snail's poison.

5 Choose the correct option.

We use *already* / *yet* in affirmative sentences.
We use *already* / *yet* in questions and negatives.

6 Look at the picture. Complete the list with the names: *Tim, Sam, Don.* The time now is 13.00.

Vaccination times	
....	12.40
Philip	12.45
Oliver	12.50
....	12.55
Mark	13.00
....	13.05

7 Put the words in order.
1 already / my medicine. / taken / have / I
2 the hospital / you / been to / have / yet?
3 has / my brother / measles. / already / had
4 yet. / have not / we / to the nurse / spoken
5 just / has / my sister / the doctor's. / gone to

We use *gone to* when a person is in a different place. We use *been to* when the person has come back from the place.
My sister isn't here. She's gone to the dentist's.
She's been to the dentist's three times this week.

➡️ See Grammar GPS, Pages 126–127

8 Make statements and questions with the present perfect and *yet* or *already.*
1 you / speak to the doctor?
2 the nurse / give me some tablets.
3 I / not have / a cold.
4 your mum / recover from her operation?
5 my brother / try the new skin cream.

Grammar: *for* and *since*

9 Read the sentences and choose the correct option.

	The sentence refers to …
1 This fact has puzzled scientists for many years.	*a period of time /* *the start of a period*
2 I've seen five people with yellow fever since March.	*a period of time /* *the start of a period*

➡️ See Grammar GPS, Pages 126–127

10 Do we use these expressions with *for* or *since*? Put the words into two groups.

one o'clock   a long time   days   a month
hours   March   Monday   a week   years
yesterday   21 January   1980

11 Complete the sentences with *for* or *since.*
1 My aunt has been in hospital .... Sunday.
2 My dad hasn't been to the doctor's .... ten years.
3 I haven't had an asthma attack .... April.
4 I've taken three painkillers .... eight o'clock.
5 My friend hasn't been to school .... two days.

12 Complete the conversation with *yet, already, just, for* and *since.*

Doctor: So, what's the matter with you?
Patient: I feel awful. I've had earache (**1**) .... three days.
Doctor: Have you got any other symptoms?
Patient: I can't hear properly, and I've had a headache (**2**) .... yesterday.
Doctor: OK. Have you taken any medicine (**3**) .... ?
Patient: Oh yes, I've (**4**) .... taken a lot of painkillers. And I've (**5**) .... tried some ear drops. That was a few minutes ago.
Doctor: Has anybody checked your ears (**6**) .... ? Let's see … Oh, what's this? It looks like the earpiece from an MP3 player!

Speaking

13 Work in pairs. Write a dialogue between a doctor and a patient. Practise the dialogue with your partner.

 If you have time
Look at the verb list on page 133. How many past participles do you know? Learn ten new ones today. Then learn ten a day until you know them all.

Reading and listening

STUDY SKILLS

1 Work in pairs. Read the introduction to the webpage. What problems do you think people will write about? Add your ideas to the list.

> school problems   bullying
> problems with friends
> eating problems   bad habits

2 ⊙ **3.3** Read and listen to the letters. Check your answers to Exercise 1.

3 ⊙ **3.4** Read and listen to the replies. Match the replies (A–D) on page 37 with the letters (1–2). There are two extra replies.

Grammar: present perfect and past simple

4 Look at the sentences from the text. When did these things happen?

1 He's drunk three cans of energy drink.

2 He went to the shop and bought chocolate.
last

3 Her mum gave her a mobile phone.
on her

4 She's had problems at school.

5 Match the events (1–4) in Exercise 4 with the times.

a at a finished time in the past

b during a period of time that includes the present

➡️➤➤ *See Grammar GPS, Pages 126–127* ➤

6 Write the present perfect or past simple of the verbs.

◆ My friend ___hasn't spoken___ to me since Monday. (not / speak)

1 We _____ to the teacher last Monday. (speak)

2 My sister _____ chocolate for three months. (not / eat)

3 I _____ on a diet last year. (go)

4 My dad _____ eating crisps in May. (give up)

5 I _____ any computer games this week. (not / play)

Teen to Teen

Do you have a problem? Are you worried about a friend? Send us an email and get help from other teenagers who have had experience of the problem.

1 I'm worried about my brother. He eats a lot of junk food. He's already eaten four doughnuts and two packets of crisps today, and it's only 11 a.m. And he's drunk three cans of energy drink. Last night, he told our mum he wasn't hungry, but he went to the shop and bought chocolate. He's always in a bad mood. I tried to talk to him about it, but he got angry with me. In fact, he hasn't spoken to me at all this week. My parents haven't noticed yet. Should I say something to them?
Damon

2 I'm fed up with my best friend. She's completely changed since her birthday. Her mum gave her a mobile phone. Before, we had a lot of fun together, shopping and meeting friends. Now she spends all her time sending texts on her mobile. She hasn't been out with us for weeks and she's not interested in doing anything. And she's had problems at school recently because she checks for messages in class. What should I do?
Maria

Working with words: adjective + preposition

7 Look at the examples. Then find the prepositions after *interested* and *angry* in the letters.

I'm fed up with my best friend.
I'm worried about my brother.

➡️➤➤ *See Working with words, Page 118* ➤

10 ⊙*3.5* Listen to the radio programme and check your ideas from Exercise 9.

CHECK IT!

11 ⊙*3.5* Listen again and choose the best answers (a–c).

1 Lance Armstrong
  a recovered from cancer.
  b is recovering from cancer.
  c hasn't recovered from cancer.
2 Lance says you should stay fit by
  a going cycling.
  b doing regular exercise.
  c being strong.
3 Lance says young people should
  a eat a lot and not exercise.
  b eat junk food, but exercise.
  c exercise and eat well.

A Your brother has a bad habit and possibly an addiction. You should help your brother – join clubs and do healthy activities with him. We did this with my sister and she stopped eating junk food.

B Your friend has a very unhealthy lifestyle. You should help her find an activity she's good at. I started cycling – and I've lost six kilos!

C Wow! There's a lot of caffeine in three cans of energy drink! Junk food is full of addictive things like sugar, salt and fat. I changed my diet when I found this out. You should talk to your parents about your brother's problem.

D Tell your parents about this. Your friend needs help. She needs to limit the time her phone is switched on. She should also do other activities, like sports, where she can't use her phone.

Speaking

8 Work in pairs. Imagine a friend has one of the problems in Exercise 1. What advice will you give him/her? Use a dictionary to help you. Then compare your ideas with a new partner.

Listening

STUDY SKILLS

9 Work in pairs. Have you heard of the cyclist Lance Armstrong? Compare your ideas with another pair.

Speaking

12 Put the words into two groups: *healthy activities* and *unhealthy activities*.

> be active   do exercise   do sports
> drink fizzy drinks   eat junk food   eat well
> lose weight   meet friends   sleep well
> eat a lot of salt   stay fit   watch a lot of TV

13 Work in pairs. Prepare six questions with the present perfect and the expressions from the Vocabulary box in Exercise 12. Work with a new partner. Ask and answer the questions.

A: *Have you eaten any junk food this week?*

B: *I've had two burgers since Sunday!*

STUDY SKILLS

Predict and check

Before you read or listen to a text, think about the topic.

1 What do you know about the topic? Write your ideas.
2 Write words in English connected to the topic.
3 When you read or listen, check for your ideas and words.

Reading and listening

1 🔊 **3.6 Read and listen to the dialogue. Who is going on holiday?**

a Lee and Jack **c** everyone

b Reem and Lauren

2 **Read the dialogue again. Find five places where somebody agrees with a statement and two places where somebody disagrees. Underline the expressions they use.**

➤➤ *See Grammar GPS, Pages 126–127* ➤

3 **Match the statements (1–5) with the responses (a–e).**

1 I'm from Egypt.

2 I'm not English.

3 I went to France last year.

4 I've been to Spain.

5 I like travelling.

a I don't.

b I haven't.

c Me too.

d Neither am I.

e So did I.

4 🔊 **3.7 Listen and repeat the *Useful expressions*.**

Useful expressions

Agreeing	Disagreeing
So am I.	I have.
Me too.	I don't.
Me neither.	
So did I.	
Neither do I.	

CHECK IT!

5 **Complete the dialogue with the correct form of the words in the box.**

be	do	have

Lee: I've never had a really serious illness.

Jack: Neither (1) _____ I. But I fell off my bike once and broke my leg.

Lee: So (2) _____ I. I was off school for two weeks.

Jack: So (3) _____ I. It was really boring.

Reem: These are great photos, Lauren. Ireland looks beautiful. It's really green! It's not like Lebanon.

Lauren: Have you been back to Lebanon recently, Reem?

Reem: No, I haven't. I'm going to see my cousins for New Year.

Lee: So am I. I'm going to China. Where are you going for New Year, Jack?

Jack: Nowhere. I'm staying at home with my family.

Lauren: Me too. I've never been abroad.

Jack: I have. I've been to France twice. Last year I went to Spain, but I was ill all week. I think it was the sun. Have you ever had sunstroke?

Lee: No, I haven't.

Lauren: Me neither.

Reem: I have. I had a really high temperature and felt terrible.

Jack: So did I. It was awful!

Reem: Lee, have you had your vaccinations yet?

Lee: Yes. I had my typhoid injection last week and got a rash all over my arm.

Lauren: Poor you! And have you packed your suitcase yet?

Lee: No, I haven't. I don't leave until the middle of December!

Reem: Neither do I. I also need to buy a new suitcase first.

Lee: I don't. I'm only taking a rucksack. I can buy everything I need in China.

Jack: Make sure you buy lots of insect repellent.

Lee: Don't worry. I'm sure my mum has thought of that! She's really worried about the mosquitoes.

Speaking

6 Work in pairs. Take turns saying the statements and agreeing. Use *So ...* and *Neither ...* .

1 I went to the dentist yesterday.

2 I've never been in hospital.

3 I was ill last week.

4 I don't like taking medicine.

5 I can run fast.

7 Prepare six statements with the present simple, past simple or present perfect for your partner to agree or disagree with. Use the prompts below or use your own ideas. Then take turns saying your statements and responding.

go / Italy	fly / helicopter
have / passport	have / a high temperature
take / malaria tablets	like / hot weather

Pronunciation: vowel sounds /æ/ and /ʌ/ in irregular verbs

8 🔘 **3.8** Listen and tick the words you hear.

1 began   begun

2 drank   drunk

3 ran   run

4 sang   sung

5 swam   swum

9 Practise saying these sentences.

1 I've never swum in the sea.

2 He sang in the concert last night.

3 Who's drunk all the orange juice?

4 She began playing tennis when she was four.

Writing: an article

1 Read the article Lauren wrote about Emma Watson for a school competition. Match the headings (a–c) with the paragraphs (1–3).

a Why this person is a good role model

b Background and achievements

c Lifestyle

2 Find examples of *although, even though* and *however* in the article. Which two expressions have the same meaning?

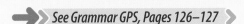 *See Grammar GPS, Pages 126–127*

3 <u>Underline</u> the correct expression or expressions in each sentence.

1 *Although / Even though / However,* he had no experience of acting, he was a huge success in his first film.

2 He has a healthy vegetarian diet. *Although / Even though / However,* he loves chocolate and cake.

3 She goes running every morning *although / even though / however* she often starts work at 7 a.m.

4 He's always busy. *Although / Even though / However,* he always has time to help other people.

4 Write notes about a role model you admire. Use the text and the paragraph headings to help you. Then write your article. Remember to include linking words from Exercise 2.

Who do you think is a good role model for young people today, and why?

1 Emma Watson is a young British actress. She's famous for her role as Hermione Granger in the *Harry Potter* films and has won many acting awards. Although Emma has been very busy filming, she's continued to study hard. She left school with excellent grades and went to an American university to study.

2 As well as acting, Emma sings and dances. She's a great hockey player and has been a skier since she was five years old. She's recently learnt to do scuba-diving. She prefers hot chocolate to coffee. She has a healthy diet and enjoys cooking. However, she usually makes cakes and biscuits!

3 I think Emma Watson is an ideal role model for girls because she's got a lot of talent, and she's sporty and academic. She hasn't become a typical celebrity, even though she's been in the media a lot. Emma Watson is a very confident and energetic person. In interviews, she's always polite, intelligent and friendly.

Reading

1 Work in pairs. What can you see in the photos?

2 **3.9** Read about the tropical disease, malaria. Match the headings (a–c) with the paragraphs (1–3).

  a The *Malaria No More* campaign

  b Theatre with a message in an African village

  c Mosquitoes and other problems

Culture

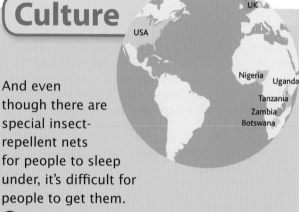

 In a village in Tanzania, an audience of children and adults is watching a performance by a group of local actors. The play is funny, dramatic and entertaining. However, it also has a serious message – it tells the story of the most dangerous animal in the world and what happened to a boy when that animal bit him. In many places in Africa, theatre and music bring news and education to isolated villages because it's difficult to buy newspapers or watch TV.

 So, which animal is the most dangerous in the world? A lion? A shark? What about a mosquito? Mosquitoes carry the parasite that causes malaria and every day malaria kills more than 3000 children in Africa. Although scientists have developed medicines to treat malaria, they are expensive.

And even though there are special insect-repellent nets for people to sleep under, it's difficult for people to get them.

3 The organisation *Malaria No More* gives mosquito nets and malaria drugs to families and it sponsors traditional health education in Africa. And in Europe and the USA, it uses the sports and entertainment industry to raise money for its activities in Africa. Forty million people have seen the special shows on *American Idol* and the campaign has raised enough money to buy 15 million mosquito nets. Sports celebrities Andy Murray and David Beckham launched the *Malaria No More* UK campaign at Wembley Stadium in London, explaining that we can save a child's life for less than the price of a football.

3 Read the text again and find these things.

1 the cause of malaria

2 two reasons why so many children die from malaria

3 two activities that *Malaria No More* does to fight malaria

4 Read the first sentence. Complete the second sentence so that it gives the same information.

1 a The actors are performing a play.

 b The actors are giving a

 ....

2 a There are medicines to treat malaria.

 b Scientists have .... medicines to treat malaria.

3 a Sometimes people can't get mosquito nets.

 b It's .... for people to get mosquito nets.

4 a The shows have had large audiences.

 b A lot of people have .... the shows.

Listening

5 ⊙ *3.10* Listen to a talk about the *Malaria No More* campaign. What can you do to help?

6 ⊙ *3.10* Listen again and complete the notes.

1 Number of people who die every year from malaria: ....

2 Cost of one bed net: $............... .

3 Ashton Kucher's donation: $............... .

4 The cost of one text donation: $............... .

Project ►►
 Write a health questionnaire for your class. Include questions about lifestyle, illnesses and accidents. Present the information in a chart or a poster.

Biology and English

Blood groups

1 Work in pairs. Discuss the answers to these questions.

1 What is blood?

2 How much blood have people got in their bodies?

3 What is a blood donor?

2 Read the text and find the answers to the questions in Exercise 1.

What does blood do?

Blood is a kind of transport system. It carries oxygen, carbon dioxide, food and other important substances around the body. There are two kinds of blood cells in the blood. Red blood cells carry oxygen. White blood cells fight infections and diseases.

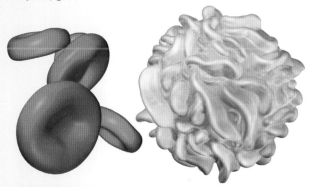

How much blood is there in a human body?

Adults have about five litres of blood. Red blood cells die after about three months, so the body makes new red blood cells all the time. When people have accidents or operations, they can lose a lot of blood. Their bodies can't make blood quickly, so they need to get blood from another person.

Is everybody's blood the same?

No, it isn't. There are some small but important differences. In the past, people sometimes died after they received blood from another person (a donor). Nobody understood this until in 1901 the Austrian scientist Karl Landsteiner discovered that there are four main types of blood. Some types of blood can mix together in the body without problems, but some combinations become solid and the blood can't move around the body. Landsteiner called the blood types A, B, AB and O.

How many blood groups are there?

Although scientists have identified more than 20 different blood types, Landsteiner's system is still useful today and his discovery has saved millions of lives.

3 Why was Landsteiner's discovery important?

Reading

HOW TO...

identify the main ideas of sections of a text
- Read the main text heading and the whole text quickly, once only.
- Read the sub-headings. Try to predict the kind of information that will follow them.
- Read the first sub-heading again and find the section of the text which matches it.
- Continue matching the sub-headings with the sections.

Important! Check the extra sub-heading to make sure it doesn't match any section.

1 Read the sub-headings from a text about 'A healthy life'. Write three words for each topic.

> **a** Make good use of your free time
> **b** Sports are for everyone
> **c** Your diet is the key to health

2 Which paragraph does sub-heading *a* match?

> **1** Eating healthy food helps you to exercise. Sugar gives you energy, but your body needs more than that. Vitamins in fruit and vegetables help your body to fight infection.

> **2** It's also important to have a variety of interests in your life. Don't spend all day in front of the TV or even reading. Get out, meet people and activate your brain.

3 Match sub-heading *b* or *c* with the other paragraph.

CHECK IT!

4 Read the text about common winter illnesses and match the correct heading (a–c) with each paragraph (1–2).

> 1 We are affected by illnesses every winter, but we can avoid some of them. A good diet and a healthy lifestyle are the key. If our bodies are strong and fit, they can resist viruses and infections.
>
> 2 One very dangerous winter illness is bronchitis. This can develop from a cold or flu, and it makes breathing difficult and painful.

> **a** How should I treat flu?
> **b** What are the symptoms of bronchitis?
> **c** How can I avoid getting ill this winter?

Language response

HOW TO...

use the correct word form
- Read the gapped text quickly, once.
- Look at the words given. Decide if they are adjectives, verbs, adverbs or nouns.
- Read each gapped sentence. Decide what changes you must make to the words.

Important! Read the whole text again when you finish.

1 What kind of words are these groups?

1 small   new   expensive   ....
2 go   be   have   ....
3 begin   find   sell   ....

2 Answer these questions about the words in Exercise 1.

1 What are their comparative forms?
2 What are their past simple forms?
3 What are their past participles?

3 Now look at this task. What changes must you make to the words in the box?

> be   go   have

> Hi Hana,
>
> I'm sorry I wasn't at home when you came. I (1) .... to visit my sister in hospital. She has (2) .... there since Monday. She (3) .... her baby on Tuesday!
>
> Jenny

4 Now complete the text in Exercise 3.

CHECK IT!

5 Complete the gapped text with the correct form of the words in the box.

> bad   buy   have

> Dear Mark,
>
> I'm sorry we (1) .... an argument last night. I was in a really bad mood. This has been the (2) .... week of my life! I've decided to make some changes. I (3) .... you a present – it's in your bedroom. See you later.
>
> Andrew

Grammar: word order with connectors

1 Put the words in the correct order to make sentences. Remember to add commas and full stops.

1 didn't go / because / outside / was raining / it / we /

2 after / stopped / however / the rain / ten / minutes /

3 so / the sun / went / the park / into / came out / we /

4 we / the grass / sat down / was / although / wet /

5 it / had / even though / a bit / was / uncomfortable /we / our picnic/

Writing practice: topic sentences and connectors of contrast, reason and result

2 Read the extract from an article about skin. Match the topic sentences (1–4) with the beginnings of the paragraphs (a–d).

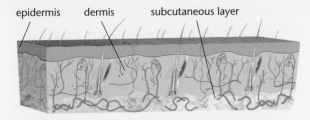

epidermis   dermis   subcutaneous layer

1 It is important to look after your skin.

2 The epidermis is made up of skin cells.

3 Skin is the largest organ in the body.

4 Without skin we would not have a sense of touch.

a _____ The skin covers and protects your bones, muscles and other organs. It also keeps your body at the correct temperature. It is made up of three different layers: the epidermis, the dermis and the subcutaneous layer, which contains fat and hair follicles.

b _____ However, the cells that you can see are all old or dead skin cells. They stay on the surface for a very short time and then fall off. New cells underneath come to the top to replace them. We lose more than 30,000 dead skin cells every minute.

c _____ The dermis contains nerve endings. They send messages to the brain when you touch something. This is how you can tell if something is soft or hard, rough or smooth, hot or cold.

d _____ Keep it clean by washing with soap and water. If your skin is cut or injured, cover it with a plaster to avoid dirt getting in and causing an infection.

3 Complete the sentences (a–e) using the connectors in the box.

| because   even though   however   so   so that |

The dermis

a The dermis also produces oil _____ your hair stays soft and healthy.

b _____ , the vessels are difficult to see, especially in young people.

c Older people have a thinner dermis, _____ you can see the vessels more easily.

d These blood vessels keep skin healthy _____ they transport nutrients to the cells.

e Your skin constantly produces sweat _____ you don't feel it.

4 Put the sentences in Exercise 3 into a logical order to make a paragraph. Now write the paragraph in your notebook.

5 Work in pairs. Write two or three possible topic sentences for the paragraph in Exercise 4 and choose the best one. Use the *Topic sentences* section in the *Writing bank* to help you.

Writing practice: paragraph writing

6 Choose a sport or activity which is good for keeping you fit and make notes about it. Include the following.

• Description of the sport/activity

• Who does it

• Why it keeps you fit

• What you need to get started

7 Organise your notes into two paragraphs and put the ideas into a logical order.

Write a topic sentence for each of your two paragraphs. (See *Tips for writing articles* in the *Writing bank*.) Then write your article.

8 Work in pairs and read your partner's article. Tick (✔) the things they have done from the list of *Tips* for *writing articles* in the *Writing bank*.

Spelling: vowel sounds

Words with /e/, /ɪ/ or /ei/ sounds Look at the list below to see which vowels and vowel combinations correspond to the sounds /e/, /ɪ/, /ei/. /e/ /ɪ/ /ei/	 bed bread bit hungry rain explanation vein
Words with /əʊ/, /ɒ/ or /ɒ:/ sounds Look at the list below to see which vowels and vowel combinations which correspond to the sounds /əʊ/, /ɒ/, /ɒ:/. /əʊ/ /ɒ/ /ɒ:/	 alone boat gone talk caught fork bought

Punctuation: capital letters

We use capital letters for:

names of people and pets:	Samantha, Ben, Naguib Mahfouz, Fluffy (the cat)
titles:	Mr, Mrs, Miss, Dr (doctor), Sir, Lady, the Queen
languages:	Arabic, English, Farsi, German
days and months:	Monday, Tuesday, January, August

Grammar: word order with connectors of contrast, reason and result

Connectors that come between two clauses

I went home because I was tired. (reason)

I was tired, so I went home. (result)

I went home so that I could relax. (reason)

I was tired but I didn't go to bed. (contrast)

I didn't go to bed, even though I was tired. (contrast)

Connectors that come at the beginning of a sentence

Although/Even though I was tired, I didn't go to bed. (contrast)

I was tired. However, I didn't go to bed. (contrast)

Note: the connectors above are all followed by a clause.

subject + verb (+object) (+ complement)

Writing practice: paragraph writing and topic sentences

Topic sentences introduce the general idea of a paragraph. The following sentences then give more detail and/or examples of the topic.

Topic sentence	**More information**
There are over 260 bones in the human body.	*Our feet are made up of over 26 small bones.* (+ more facts and figures)
Bones come in all shapes and sizes.	*There are large, flat bones such as the skull or shoulder blades.* (+ more types of bone)

Many writers use questions:

Did you know that there are over 260 bones in the human body?
Have you ever been on a walking holiday?

Connectors of contrast work well in topic sentences:

However, bones and joints can wear out, so it is important to keep them strong.

Although you do not need any special equipment, a good pair of shoes is essential.

Writing practice: tips for writing articles

- Write a short, interesting title.
- Make sure your topic sentences give a clear idea of the subject of each paragraph.
- Make sure that the ideas in your paragraph are related to the topic sentence.
- Make sure that the topic sentence of the first paragraph is interesting. This is the first sentence of the whole article so it should grab the reader's attention.
- Use connectors to link your ideas.
- Go back and read your title – you may want to change it.

GRAMMAR
Learn about the present simple and past simple passive with *by*, and quantifiers: *all, most, much, many, a lot / lots, some, few, little* + nouns.

SKILLS
Read about the environment, the Arabian oryx, and symbolic animals.

Listen to an interview about birds, and a journalist talking about elephants.

Write a description of a place.

COMMUNICATE!
Give and check information.

VOCABULARY
Learn words for natural disasters and wild animals.

Work with adjective + noun combinations, and words with two meanings.

Natural disasters	
avalanche	sandstorm
drought	storm
earthquake	tornado
flood	tsunami
heatwave	volcanic
hurricane	eruption
lightning	wildfire
mudslide	

CARING FOR THE PLANET

1 Work in pairs. Look at the photo. Where do you think it is? Why? Do the natural disasters in the Vocabulary box happen in your country? Which natural disasters or extreme weather have you experienced?

2 ⊙ *4.1* Listen to four news stories. Write the numbers (1–4) next to four natural disasters in the Vocabulary box.

3 ⊙ *4.1* Listen again and tick the words you hear.

fire	wind	water	rain	drought	snow
temperature	lightning	lava	ash	smoke	

4 Work in pairs. Ask and answer the questions.

1 Which natural disasters are the most frightening / dangerous / destructive? Why?

2 Have you seen any of these things on the news? Which ones?

3 Which natural disasters have you experienced? Where? When?

Reading and listening

1 Work in pairs. Read the questions (1–4) on the webpage. Discuss your answers.

2 ⊙ **4.2** Read and listen to the webpage. How many answers did you get right?

Speaking

3 Read the last part of the webpage. Discuss your answers with your partner. Think of three things you can do to reduce your *carbon footprint* – the damage you do to the environment.

Working with words: adjective + noun

4 Look at the examples. Then find two adjectives before *activity* in the webpage.

natural + disaster = natural disaster

global + warming = global warming

➤➤ *See Working with words, Page 119* ➤

ENVIRONMENT DAY

Try our quiz on the natural events and human activities that change our environment. Then calculate **your** impact on the environment.

1 How are earthquakes sometimes caused?
   a by volcanoes   **b** by tsunamis   **c** by human activity

2 Are volcanoes the most dangerous natural disaster?

3 What's the most important environmental problem today?
   a floods and fire   **b** pollution from waste
   c global warming

4 Where do greenhouse gases come from?

1 a) and **c)** An earthquake is a violent movement in the Earth's crust. Sometimes, the movement is caused by natural volcanic activity. However, the 2008 Sichuan earthquake in China was caused by human activity – the construction of the Zipingpu dam. On the other hand, tsunamis are often the result of an earthquake under the sea.

2 No. Most volcanoes aren't as destructive as earthquakes. And sometimes, new land is formed by volcanoes. For example, the Canary Islands were created by volcanic eruptions millions of years ago.

3 c) It's true that floods and fires destroy enormous areas of land. And the things we throw away, from plastic bags to old computers, don't disappear. Some are recycled, but most are dumped on rubbish tips. But our biggest problem is global warming because every living thing is affected by temperature changes in the environment.

4 In the past, greenhouse gases only occurred naturally. They weren't produced by human activity until the industrial age. The two main sources are burning fuel and deforestation. For example, when trees in the Amazon forest are cut down, the wood isn't used. It's burnt. More than 20 per cent of all greenhouse gases are produced as a result of deforestation.

WHAT ABOUT YOU?

In a normal week,

how much ...	how many ...
rubbish does your family throw away?	plastic bags do you use?
plastic does your family recycle?	cans do you throw away?
paper do you waste?	bottles do you recycle?

Calculate your carbon footprint here.

Grammar: passive

5 Look at the examples. <u>Underline</u> six more present simple passive verbs in the webpage.

How are earthquakes caused?

The movement is caused by natural volcanic activity.

6 Complete the sentence with the words in the box. <u>Underline</u> the cause and (circle) the result.

> earthquakes   tsunamis

_____ are caused by _____ .

We use *by* when we want to say who or what does or causes the action.

7 Complete the table with the words in the box.

> is   isn't   are   aren't

	Present simple passive
Affirmative	The movement is caused by natural volcanic activity. Many trees **(1)** _____ cut down each year.
Negative	The wood **(2)** _____ used. Earthquakes **(3)** _____ caused by tsunamis.
Questions	**(4)** _____ the plastic recycled? How are earthquakes caused?

We make the passive with the verb *be* + past participle. We use *was* and *were* to make the past simple passive.

➤➤➤ *See Grammar GPS, Page 127* ➤

8 Complete the past simple passive sentences.

1 The earthquake in 2008 _____ by human activity. (cause)

2 The Canary Islands _____ millions of years ago. (create)

3 In 2009, 60 per cent of domestic rubbish _____ . (not / recycle)

4 Before 1750, greenhouse gases _____ by man. (not / produce)

5 When _____ plastic _____ for the first time? (make)

6 _____ the trees _____ in the hurricane last year? (blow down)

➤➤➤ *See Grammar GPS, Page 127* ➤

CHECK IT!

9 Choose the correct option.

1 Lightning *kills* / *is killed* more people than tornadoes.

2 Most avalanches *start* / *are started* by people.

3 Mount Etna *didn't erupt* / *wasn't erupted* last year.

4 Trees *cut down* / *were cut down* to make new farmland.

5 The forest fire *didn't put out* / *wasn't put out* until the temperature fell.

10 Write the verbs in the present simple or past simple passive.

An enormous quantity of oil (**1** need) _____ to produce plastic bags and bottles. In the process, greenhouse gases (**2** release) _____ . More than 200 billion litres of bottled water (**3** sell) _____ last year. Most of these bottles (**4** not / recycle) _____ after the water (**5** drink) _____ . They (**6** throw away) _____ . After many years, waste plastic (**7** break down) _____ into tiny pieces by the weather. Sometimes, it (**8** eat) _____ by birds and other animals. This usually kills them.

Speaking

11 Work in pairs. Write questions with the sentences and the question words.

1 Plastic is made from oil. (what)

2 450 million plastic bags are used each month in the UK. (how many)

3 Plastic bags were banned in San Francisco in 2007. (when)

4 Paper is made from trees. (what)

5 One million tonnes of paper are recycled each year in the UK. (how much)

6 Paper was invented in China. (where)

12 Work with a new partner. Ask and answer your questions from Exercise 11. Take turns.

> **If you have time**
> Which is the odd one out in each list? Why? Write more lists for a partner.
> 1 hurricane   lightning   tornado   volcano
> 2 rain   snow   water   wind
> 3 ash   flood   lava   smoke
> 4 gas   glass   paper   plastic

Speaking

1 Work in pairs and complete the sentences with the animals. More than one answer is possible.

bats	crocodiles	deer	dolphins	eagles
falcons	foxes	gazelles	goats	hares	ibises
leopards	lizards	lynx	oryx	owls	storks
tigers	wolves	snakes		

1 _____ fly at night.

2 _____ live in rivers and lakes.

3 _____ are predators – they eat smaller animals.

4 _____ are often poisonous.

5 _____ and _____ are very rare.

2 Have you ever seen these animals? Which ones? Where? Tell your partner.

Listening

CHECK IT!

3 ○**4.3** **Listen to the interview. What is the interview about?**

a hunting wild birds in the Middle East

b protecting rare birds in the wild

c tracking wild birds in Egypt

4 ○**4.3** **Listen again. Put the sentences in the correct order.**

a The adult birds were tracked by satellite to Ethiopia.

b The young birds were lost during migration.

c Seven ibises were found by researchers in Syria.

d Six ibises were donated by Turkey.

e Six birds were hatched.

Reading and listening

STUDY SKILLS

5 Read the text quickly. Your teacher will time you. Did you get a general idea of what the text is about? Compare your ideas with your partner.

6 ○**4.4** Read and listen to the text. Were your ideas correct?

The Arabian oryx

The Arabian oryx is a symbolic animal. Its beauty has inspired artists and poets for centuries. Some people believe that the legend of the unicorn originated from the Arabian oryx. There aren't many wild Arabian oryx today. If you want to see them in their natural environment, you need to go to the Mahazat as-Sayd Protected Area, Saudi Arabia's largest nature reserve. However, 40 years ago, there were no Arabian oryx in the wild.

Centuries ago, the Arabian oryx inhabited most of the Middle East, including Egypt, Iraq and Jordan. By 1914, they were only found in the deserts and grasslands of Saudi Arabia. This area was full of wild animals such as gazelles, wolves, hyenas, jackals and oryx. They were often hunted for food and for sport. In the 1930s, the Arabian oryx was hunted by men who used fast cars and large rifles. The animals had little chance of escape. The last wild Arabian oryx was killed in 1972. Fortunately, a few of the last Arabian oryx were captured in 1962 and bred in captivity. In 1982, the first Arabian oryx were

7 **Working with words: Words with two meanings**

Find these words in the text and choose the correct definition.

little = **a** not a lot
b small in size

quarter = **a** an area
b one of four equal parts

See Working with words, Page 119

CHECK IT!

8 Read the text again. Are the sentences true or false?

1 The Arabian oryx is the subject of many paintings and poems.

2 There aren't any wild Arabian oryx in Saudi Arabia today.

3 Forty years ago, there were many wild Arabian oryx.

4 The oryx in Oman are protected from hunters.

5 The number of wild Arabian oryx in the desert has increased.

reintroduced into the wild in Oman. However, there isn't much protection in the area. Lots of animals have been killed by hunters.

In 1989, the Saudi Wildlife Commission created the Mahazat as-Sayd Protected Area. A year later, 72 Arabian oryx were reintroduced to the area and recent data shows that there are now 400 Arabian oryx living there. In 1995, a group of 121 Arabian oryx were released into a protected area of the Empty Quarter. The reintroduction of the Arabian oryx in Saudi Arabia is an environmental success story. Before 1986, the Arabian oryx was classified as extinct in the wild. It is still an endangered animal, but today there are over 1,000 Arabian oryx living in their natural habitats.

Grammar: many, much, few, little

9 **Look at the examples. Then choose the correct options.**

There aren't many wild Arabian oryx today.

A few of the last Arabian oryx were captured in 1962.

The animals had little chance of escape.

There isn't much protection in the area.

We use *many* and *few* with *countable / uncountable* nouns.

We use *much* and *little* with *countable / uncountable* nouns.

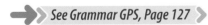 **See Grammar GPS, Page 127**

10 **Read the first sentence. Complete the second sentence with *few* or *little*.**

1 a There weren't many animals.

  b There were _____ animals.

2 a We didn't have much time.

  b We had _____ time.

3 a We don't have much information.

  We have _____ information.

4 a I didn't see many people.

  b I saw _____ people.

5 a There wasn't much pollution.

  b There was _____ pollution.

 We normally use *much* and *many* in negative sentences and questions.

11 **Choose the correct options.**

1 Are there *much / many* endangered species in *Saudi Arabia*?

2 Scientists found *few / little* tigers in the area.

3 How *much / few* snow fell last night?

4 We didn't see *much / many* eagles.

5 *Much / Many* of the animals have survived.

12 **Find the words in the box in the text. Then complete the table.**

few	little	lots	most

100%	all (of)
	a lot of , **(1)** _____ ,
	(2) _____ (of)
50%	some (of)
	(3) _____ , **(4)** _____
0%	none

Speaking

13 **Complete the sentences. Then compare your answers with your partner's.**

1 I've been to _____ national parks.

2 There are _____ wild animals where I live.

3 There's _____ pollution in our area.

4 There are _____ zoos near here.

5 There's _____ development in this area.

STUDY SKILLS

When you read a text quickly for the first time, follow the strategy below. It will help you to get a general idea of the topic.

1 Read the title.

2 Read the first line of the first paragraph.

3 Scan the rest of the paragraph so that your eyes move quickly over the text.

4 Read the last line of the paragraph.

5 Repeat steps 2 to 4 for the other paragraphs.

Giving and checking information

Reading and listening

1 4.5 **Read and listen to the dialogue. What are the subjects of Jack, Lauren and Lee's projects?**

2 Read the dialogue again. <u>Underline</u> the questions. Which questions ask for information? Which questions check information?

3 Lee and Jack use three expressions to show they are not sure about things. What are they?

Lauren: Hi, Jack. Where's Reem?

Jack: She's in the library. We're doing our science project. We're doing 'solar power', but I don't know much about it.

Lauren: Oh, neither do I. Do you have to hand it in next week?

Jack: I don't think so. I think it's for the end of term.

Lauren: Is it? My project is for next week.

Jack: What's it about?

Lauren: It's about recycling. Do you know how many recycled bottles are needed to make a jacket?

Jack: I have no idea.

Lauren: Twenty-five.

Jack: Is that possible? Are you sure?

Lauren: Yes, I'm sure ... Lee told me. You know he's really into science.

Jack: Oh yes ... hey, Lee! What do you know about solar power?

Lee: Actually, I can tell you a lot about solar power. My brother's studying environmental science at university and he's told me a lot about it.

Jack: Really? Is he coming home soon?

Lee: Next week, probably. But I can give you his email address and you can send him a message.

Jack: Great! What's your project, Lee?

Lee: Oh, it's about an animal rescue centre. I've decided to work there at weekends – as a volunteer.

Jack: What about your plans to be a doctor?

Lee: Maybe I'll be a vet instead.

4 ○ **4.6** Listen and repeat the *Useful expressions.* Focus on your intonation.

Useful expressions

What do you know about solar power?
Do you know how many recycled bottles are needed to make a jacket?
I can tell you a lot about solar power.
Next week, probably.
Maybe I'll be a vet instead.

Is that possible?	I have no idea.
Are you sure?	I don't think so.
I don't know much about it.	Yes, I'm sure.

---

5 Match the sentences (1–4) with the responses (a–e). There is one extra response.

1 Are you sure?

2 Can you make plastic from plants?

3 Look at this – a car powered by water!

4 What do you know about recycling?

a I don't know much about it.

b I don't think so.

c Is that possible?

d Yes, I'm sure.

e Pollution, probably.

Writing: a description of a place

1 Read Jack's article and match the headings (a–c) with the paragraphs (1–3).

a A special place

b General information and history

c Things to do and see

2 Underline *also, for example, including, like, such as* and *too* in the article.

3 Choose the correct option.

There are many areas of natural beauty in Britain. (**1**) *For example / Such as,* you can visit the Lake District and the Cairngorms, where there are beautiful mountains. Snowdonia, in Wales, is (**2**) *too / also* mountainous. In these places, you can do lots of outdoor activities, (**3**) *like / also* mountain climbing and sailing. You can go hiking (**4**) *such as / too.* There is a lot of accommodation, (**5**) *including / also* camping, chalets, bed and breakfast or hotels.

4 Write a description of your favourite place. Write three paragraphs. Use Jack's article to help you and use the linking words in Exercise 2.

Speaking

6 Work in pairs. Talk about the topics in the box. Use the *Useful expressions.* Begin each conversation with *What do you know about … ?*

pop music   the solar system national parks in our country pandas   British football   India

Pronunciation: the letters 'o' and 'oo', the vowel sounds /ʊ/, /uː/ and /ʌ/

7 ○ **4.7** Listen and repeat these words.

blood   book   cool   does   flood foot   good   move   school   some

8 ○ **4.7** Listen again and complete the table.

/ʊ/	/uː/	/ʌ/
book	cool	blood

My favourite place: Dovedale

1 Dovedale is a beautiful valley in the Peak District, Derbyshire. Dovedale was formed 350 million years ago from limestone rock. During two ice ages, the rock was cut into strange and amazing shapes by the melting ice, and caves like Dove Holes were formed.

2 There are lots of things to do and see in Dovedale. For example, you can go hill walking or trout fishing in the River Dove. You can visit the caves too. In the past, many of the caves, such as Reynard's Cave, were used as shelters. There is also a lot of wildlife, including rare plants and birds. In 2006, Dovedale became a National Nature Reserve.

3 My favourite part of Dovedale is the Stepping Stones. During the summer, when the water is low, you can cross the stones or paddle in the river. It's a great place for a picnic, and to relax and enjoy the scenery.

Reading

1 Work in pairs. Which words can you use to describe the animals in the photos? Use a dictionary.

dangerous	domesticated	endangered	pets
protected	free	symbolic	wild

2 🔘 **4.8** Work in pairs. Do you think these sentences are true or false? Why? / Why not? Then read about animals in India.

1 Elephants are wild animals found in Africa.

2 Cows live on farms, and they produce milk and meat.

3 Tigers are common in Asia.

3 Read the text again. Find three reasons why these animals are important in Indian life.

4 Match the adjectives with the nouns. How many more adjectives can you think of to go with *animal*?

Indian	working	protected	endangered
animal	culture	day	species

Culture   India

India is a huge country with many different types of habitat, including deserts, forests and the highest mountains in the world – the Himalayas. It has over 65,000 species of animals, such as elephants, rhinos and bears. And it is the only country in the world with both lions and tigers.

Animals are important in Indian culture and some are treated in a special way. For example, a lot of the elephants aren't wild. They are domesticated. They aren't kept as pets, but as working animals. Every working elephant has its own carer, a boy called a *mahout*. An elephant and its mahout meet for the first time when they are both young, and they grow up together. In fact, their relationship continues for the rest of the elephant's life – perhaps 40 years. Lots of elephants work in the forest, moving heavy trees when they are cut down. Some give rides to tourists, or carry people during ceremonies and festivals. Mahouts usually take excellent care of their elephants, feeding them well and giving them a bath at the end of the working day.

Another special animal in India is the cow. Cows are protected animals, so they aren't kept on farms or killed for food although people do use their milk. So in India you can often see cows walking around towns and cities, and nobody tries to control them. If they sit down in the middle of the road, people simply drive around them!

The Bengal tiger is a symbol of strength and health in India – in fact, it's the national animal. However, the tiger population has fallen and now it's an endangered species. Luckily, things are beginning to change: the *Kids for Tigers* campaign is supported by more than a million children, and the number of tigers in one important park – the Panna Tiger Reserve – has increased.

CHECK IT!

5 **Complete the description of the elephant in the photo on page 52.**

The elephant in the photo is at a festival in Jaipur. It is wearing a headdress which is (1) _____ of silver. It has a large, brightly-coloured cover (2) _____ its back. There is a young trainer on its back, and he is wearing a turban and beautiful (3) _____ .
The photo was taken by a tourist on holiday in Jaipur.

1 a make   **b** made
   c making
2 a on   **b** in
   c behind
3 a wears   **b** clothe
   c clothes

Listening

6 *4.9* **Listen to a journalist talking about elephants. Where is he?**

a at a festival
b at a palace
c at a health camp

7 *4.9* **Listen again and choose the correct option (a–c).**

1 How long do the elephants stay at Punnathur?
   a one day
   b one week
   c one month
2 Who washes the elephants' faces?
   a a junior trainer
   b a senior trainer
   c another elephant
3 What happens after the elephants' bath?
   a they have dinner
   b they play
   c they go to sleep
4 Where do these elephants usually live?
   a in the jungle
   b in palaces
   c in temples

Biology and English
Endangered species

1 **Work in pairs. Discuss these questions.**

1 What was the dodo and what happened to it?
2 Why do animals become endangered?

2 **Read the article and check your answers.**

Most people have heard of the dodo. It lived on the island of Mauritius, in the Indian Ocean, and it became extinct in 1681. Why did dodos disappear? There are several reasons and they are all relevant today, more than 300 years later.

Firstly, the dodo was a bird, but it was large and heavy, and it couldn't fly. It lost the ability to fly because there were no predators on Mauritius. Secondly, the dodo wasn't afraid of humans because there weren't any people on Mauritius until 1600. So, when people arrived with monkeys, cats and other animals, the dodo's habitat changed very quickly. Dodo nests and eggs were destroyed by the new predators, and the adult birds were probably shot or caught. The forest was changed too, by people who started to farm the land.

Today, animals are threatened by the same dangers – human activity and habitat destruction. In Asia, people have moved into new areas and there is less wild habitat for tigers. In Africa, changes in the way land is used mean that there is much less forest for mountain gorillas. And all around the world, different species are threatened by the effects of climate change, from polar bears in the Arctic to coral reefs on the equator.

3 **Do you think it is important to try and save species from extinction? Why? / Why not?**

Project
Find out about wild animals in your country. What is their natural habitat? Are they protected? Are any of them endangered?

Reading

1 Read the sentences. What topic have they got in common?

a The resort is opening new ski runs this winter.

b He has skied on every mountain in Europe.

c They were all experienced skiers.

2 Read the text quickly. What is it about (a–c)?

a Skiing accidents that happened in 2009

b A famous European skier

c A new ski resort in France

Skiing disasters on Europe's mountains

2009 was a bad year for avalanches in the Alps. Three skiers were killed in separate accidents in France and Switzerland. (**1**) _____ Scientists say the avalanches were caused by sudden increases in temperature.

3 Which sentence from Exercise 1 fits the gap in the text in Exercise 2?

CHECK IT!

4 Read the text and match the sentences (a–c) with the gaps (1–2). There is one extra sentence.

Many homeless after earthquakes

There were several major earthquakes last year. (**1**) _____ In Japan, two large cities in the north of the country were affected. Many buildings were destroyed. People have moved to other areas to look for new homes. (**2**) _____ Scientists say more earthquakes are expected.

a Some have gone to live with their families in other parts of Japan.

b Volcanoes often erupt at this time of year.

c They hit countries including China and Japan.

Language response

1 Look at the picture. Answer the questions.

1 What can you see?

2 Where are they?

3 What are they doing?

2 Read the description and think of a word or words for each gap.

In the photo, there are two men and a gorilla in a national park. One man (**1**) _____ and the other man is sitting on the ground. The gorilla is sitting (**2**) _____ this man and it's looking at him. The gorilla seems friendly and interested (**3**) _____ the man.

CHECK IT!

3 Read the options for each gap and choose the correct answers.

1 a stands **b** are standing **c** was standing

2 a under **b** behind **c** in front of

3 a on **b** with **c** in

Writing Insights

Spelling: silent consonants and silent *e*

1 Correct the spelling mistakes in these sentences. Look at *Spelling* in the *Writing bank*.

1 He cut his rist with a nife.
2 There's a casle on the iland.
3 I ofen lisen to music in the car.
4 Coud you help me rite this letter?
5 Do you now anything about sychology?

2 Add the missing *e* to each of these words.

1 belive
2 carfully
3 definatly
4 injuris
5 intresting

6 recives
7 disliks
8 temperatur
9 vegtable
10 worrid

Punctuation: capital letters

3 Which words need a capital letter? Rewrite them.

health centre	heathrow airport	liverpool football club
nature reserve	port	the united nations
the burj khalifa	sports club	yellowstone national park
university	upton high school	asia
african elephant	egypt	london

Grammar: the agent in passive sentences

4 Cross out the agent in these sentences where it is not needed.

1 In our experiment, the chemicals were mixed by us in the laboratory.
2 The animals were released into the wild by experienced researchers.
3 Flowers were used by someone to decorate the room.
4 John was treated in hospital by the best doctors in the country.
5 His books have been translated by translators into many languages.

Writing: giving examples

5 Complete these sentences by giving examples using the words in brackets ( ).

1 My brother has visited many countries in Europe _____ (including)
2 Many people are vaccinated against common illnesses _____ (such as)
3 Green vegetables _____ are full of vitamins and minerals. (such as)
4 A lot of rubbish can be recycled. You can _____ (for example)
5 Natural disasters can be caused by extreme weather. _____ (for example)

6 Make notes about the country or region where you live. Include the following:

• location and size
• towns and cities
• mountains, deserts, rivers etc
• climate
• interesting facts, famous buildings, important historical events

7 Organise your notes into two or three paragraphs. Then look at your notes and decide what the main topic of each paragraph is. Write a short heading for each paragraph.

8 Now write your article. Use the *Useful expressions* in the *Writing bank*. Remember to write a topic sentence for each paragraph and give examples. Give your article a title: the name of your country or your region.

9 Work in pairs. Read your partner's article and put a tick (✓) or a cross (✗) next to the points below. Put two ticks if they've done a really good job.

____ used capital letters correctly?
____ included examples?
____ written short, informative headings?
____ chosen good topic sentences?
____ joined his/her ideas with connectors?
____ written an interesting article?

Spelling: silent consonants

Position of silent consonants

Silent consonants often come before another consonant:

b before *t*: debt, doubt   *p* before *s*: psychology
k before *n*: know, knife   *s* before *l*: island, isle
l before *d*: could, should   *w* before *r*: wrist, write

Silent *t*

t is silent in these letter combinations:

sten: fasten   listen   Also in: often   soften
stl: castle   whistle

Silent *e*

If a root word ends in *e*, it is not pronounced before suffixes and verb endings beginning with a consonant or with *y*:

brave	bravely	shine	shiny
cure	cures	use	useful
separate	separately		

Exceptions to the rule

Adjectives ending in *able* and *ible* drop the final *e* before adding *y* to make an adverb:

comfortable   comfortably   incredible   incredibly

Note: before suffixes beginning with a vowel (*ed* and *ing*) the final *e* is deleted:

come	coming	save	saved

e is written but not pronounced separately with plural nouns ending in *ies*:

laboratory	laboratories	mystery	mysteries

e is not pronounced separately in *ie* and *ei*:

believe   caffeine   receipt

In words where there is an *e* before and after a single consonant, the *e* is sometimes not pronounced:

interest   vegetable

Punctuation: capital letters in names

Specific buildings and organisations

We capitalise the names of specific buildings and organisations.

Saudi Wildlife Commission   Leap Fitness Centre
The Taj Mahal   Barcelona Airport

Places

We capitalise the names of the following places:

cities, countries, islands, continents (and parts of continents), planets (but not the sun or the earth).
Istanbul   Greece   the Isle of Man
the Antarctic   Central Asia   Saturn

Rivers, lakes, seas and oceans

the Thames   Lake Geneva   the Red Sea

Deserts and mountain ranges

the Andes   the Gobi Desert
Note: there is no capital letter for *the*.

Animals

With the names of animals, we only add a capital letter to nationality adjectives or if a person has given their name to a species.
Bengal tiger   Magellanic penguin

Grammar: the agent in passive sentences

You need to mention the agent when the information about the agent is important. You often do this when you want to talk about the agent, and what they did, in the next sentence.

The tennis champion was beaten by a new player. The young Australian, Chris Simms, is only 15 years old. He has not competed in an international championship before.

You do not mention the agent when:

you are describing processes and scientific experiments.

Then, the bottles are put into boxes.

the agent is 'people in general'.

Wild foxes are often seen in cities and towns.

the agent is not known.

All the posters have been taken down!

the agent is not important.

Tania was given the best part in the play.

we already know who the agent is or it's obvious who the agent is.

I went to the dentist's. I was told I needed a filling.

Writing: giving examples

The following expressions can be used to introduce examples. They are separated from the rest of the sentence with commas.

Paris is famous for its art. For example, you can visit its museums, including the Louvre and the Musée d'Orsay. In areas such as Montmartre, you can see artists at work in the street.

Useful expressions: describing a country or region

France is a large country in Western Europe.
It is famous for its food and palaces.
The capital city is Paris.
It has borders with Belgium, Germany, Italy, Spain and Switzerland.
It has coastlines on the English Channel and the Mediterranean in the south.
The weather is warm and sunny in the south.
There are lots of mountains as well as rivers.
France has an interesting history.
You can see old buildings and castles all over France.
My favourite part of the country is the south coast.

Grammar consolidation
Present perfect and past simple

See Grammar GPS, Pages 127–128

Present perfect and past simple with *for* and *since*

We use for and *since* with the present perfect. We can also use *for* with the past simple.

1 Complete the sentences with *for* or *since*.

1 I've played tennis four times _____ May.

2 We played tennis _____ two hours, then we went swimming.

3 I haven't played tennis _____ three weeks. Let's have a game.

4 My sister is a vegetarian. She hasn't eaten meat _____ five years.

5 My mum hasn't drunk any coffee _____ New Year's Eve.

6 My dad drank coffee every day _____ ten years.

Present perfect and past simple with time expressions

We use the past simple with time expressions for a finished time in the past. We use the present perfect with time expressions for a period of time that includes the present.

2 Choose the correct verb forms.

1 We *didn't watch / haven't watched* TV last week.

2 I *went / have been* to the doctor's twice this month.

3 My friend *broke / has broken* his leg yesterday.

4 I *wasn't / haven't been* ill last year.

5 We *did / have done* lots of homework this week.

3 Choose the correct option.

1 We've done a lot of cycling *this year / last year.*

2 I've been ill *on Monday / since Monday.*

3 We saw two eagles *in June / since June.*

4 I didn't go to the park *on Sunday / since Sunday.*

5 We were here *at one o'clock / since one o'clock.*

4 Write the sentences in Exercise 3 with the other time expression. Change the verb forms.

Present perfect and past simple without time expressions

Sometimes we don't use a time expression. The time period is clear from the information we give.

5 Read the sentences and decide if the time period is in the past or includes the present. Then choose the correct option.

1 Vincent van Gogh *was / has been* an incredible artist.

2 Celine Dion *made / has made* great albums.

3 Michael Phelps *won / has won* eight gold medals at the Beijing Olympics.

6 Write the correct form of the verbs: present perfect or past simple.

Alexander Fleming (**1** win) _____ the Nobel prize in 1945. He (**2** discover) _____ the antibiotic, penicillin. Since then, scientists (**3** develop) _____ different kinds of antibiotics. Antibiotics (**4** save) _____ many people's lives.

Other uses of the present perfect and past simple

We use the present perfect (**a**) to give news. We use the past simple (**b**) to ask for or give details about the news, or (**c**) to talk about a sequence of events.

7 <u>Underline</u> the present perfect and past simple in the dialogue. Match the sentences with the uses (a, b and c) above.

Adil: I've made some popcorn. Do you want some?

Bilal: Oh, yes please. How did you make it?

Adil: I put the packet in the microwave for 30 seconds! Then I opened the packet and emptied it into the bowl.

8 Complete the dialogue with the present perfect or past simple of the verbs.

Eve: (**1** take) _____ you ever _____ this painkiller, *AcheAway*?

Jo: Yes, I (**2** take) _____ one when I (**3** have) _____ earache last month.

Eve: (**4** help) _____ it _____ ?

Jo: Well, I (**5** make) _____ some hot chocolate, (**6** take) _____ the tablet and (**7** fall) _____ asleep. When I (**8** wake up) _____ , I (**9** feel) _____ better.

Vocabulary

1 **Complete the dialogue.**

A: I feel awful. I've got **(1)** a h_____ ,
(2) a s_____ t_____ and
(3) e_____ .

B: Maybe it's **(4)** f_____ . You should take
(5) a p_____ .

1 mark per item: …/5 marks

2 **Write the activities.**

My family is very healthy. We always eat
(1) w_____ and we do **(2)** e_____
every day. We're very **(3)** a_____ . And we
don't **(4)** s_____ or eat **(5)** j_____
f_____ .

1 mark per item: …/5 marks

3 **Complete the sentences with words about the
environment.**

1 A v_____ has erupted in Italy.
2 After no rain, there was a d_____ .
3 Cars and traffic cause p_____ .
4 Things we throw away are r_____ .
5 Global w_____ is a big problem.

1 mark per item: …/5 marks

4 **Write the animals.**

1 _____
2 _____
3 _____
4 _____
5 _____

1 mark per item: …/5 marks

5 **Complete the sentences.**

1 I'm not afraid _____ spiders.
2 My friend is really bad _____ maths.
3 At our school, _____ is from twelve
thirty to one o'clock.
4 Lions and tigers are _____ animals.
5 My best _____ 's name is Karima.

1 mark per item: …/5 marks

Grammar

6 **Make statements and questions with the
present perfect.**

1 I / just / arrive home.
2 you / take the medicine / yet?
3 We / already / see two eagles.
4 your dad / speak to the doctor / yet?
5 I / already / eat my lunch.

1 mark per item: …/5 marks

7 **Complete the sentences with *for* or *since*.**

1 I haven't been to the doctor's _____ last year.
2 My friend has lived here _____ a month.
3 My mum has been a vegetarian _____ 1998.
4 I've read two books _____ yesterday.
5 My dad hasn't eaten crisps _____ March.

1 mark per item: …/5 marks

8 **Complete the sentences with the present
perfect or past simple form of the verbs.**

1 I _____ any coffee today. (not / drink)
2 I _____ a cold in January. (have)
3 We _____ two exams this week. (do)
4 Mount Etna _____ three times last
summer. (erupt)
5 My friend _____ ill since Monday. (be)

1 mark per item: …/5 marks

9 **Complete the sentences with the present simple
or past simple passive form of the verbs.**

1 Glass bottles _____ in our town.
(recycle)
2 Plastic _____ from oil. (make)
3 The area _____ by a tsunami in
2011. (destroy)
4 The species _____ until 2009.
(not / discover)
5 All the tickets _____ last week. (sell)

1 mark per item: …/5 marks

10 **Choose the correct option.**

1 There *was / were* few animals in the desert.
2 There weren't *many / much* people at school.
3 We saw *much / lots of* birds.
4 *Was / Were* there any pollution in the river?
5 There are *few / little* endangered species here.

1 mark per item: …/5 marks

Communicate!

11 Complete the responses.

1 'I like cycling.'
  'Me ....'
2 'I can speak English.'
  'So .... I.'
3 'I don't eat chocolate.'
  'Me ....'
4 'I was ill yesterday.'
  'So .... I.'
5 'I've never seen a lion.'
  'Neither .... I.'

2 marks per item: …/10 marks

12 Match the sentences (1–5) with the responses (a–e).

1 What do you know about eagles?
2 This is a solar-powered computer.
3 I need some information on recycling.
4 Are you sure?
5 How do you make popcorn?

a I have no idea.
b Yes, I'm sure.
c I don't know much about them.
d Is that possible?
e I can tell you a lot about it.

2 marks per item: …/10 marks

13 Is the sound the same as (S) or different from (D) *run*?

1 come ....
2 drunk ....
3 cool ....
4 blood ....
5 move ....
6 book ....
7 sung ....
8 good ....
9 shoot ....
10 flood ....

1 mark per item: …/10 marks

14 Match the two parts of the sentences.

1 Although I like chocolate,
2 The park has wild animals,
3 Although I studied a lot,
4 We recycle everything,
5 There's lots to do,

a I don't often eat it.
b I failed the exam.
c including paper.
d like sailing and climbing.
e like tigers and leopards.

2 marks per item: …/10 marks

15 Complete the paragraph with these words.

all of	also	even though	for example
however	lots of	no	such as	than	too

What do you do to protect the environment?

There are (**1**) .... things we can do for the environment. (**2**) ...., we can recycle (**3**) .... the glass we use. We can recycle plastic (**4**) .... We can (**5**) .... buy recycled products, (**6**) .... paper. (**7**) .... recycling uses energy, it's better (**8**) .... using new resources. (**9**) ...., the most important thing is to consume less. We have to try and save our planet! We have (**10**) .... alternative.

1 mark per item: …/10 marks

Total: …/100

I can...

Tick (✔) what you can do.

	★★★★★	★★★	★
I can agree and disagree.			
I can give information.			
I can check information.			

True story: The real-life Indiana Jones

1 Work in pairs. Look at the photos. What can you see? Use the words in the box to help you.

> adventure   ancient city   archaeology
> dangerous   discovery   Egypt   film
> images   pyramids   satellite   space

2 Read the text quickly. Can you find any of the words in Exercise 1?

3 Read the text again and answer the questions.

  1 What did Dr Parcak discover in 2011?

  2 How did Dr Parcak make her discovery?

  3 What surprised her about the discovery?

  4 Why is she excited about the pyramids at Saqqara?

5 In what other ways has space-archaeology been used?

6 Who will take part in future excavations?

4 Finds words with these meanings in the text.

  1 the place where ancient cities or buildings are found

  2 very surprised

  3 to dig the earth

  4 very old objects

5 Work in groups. Do you think that Dr Parcak's job is exciting? Do you think that more young people will become interested in archaeology in the future? Why/Why not?

In 2011, American Egyptologist Dr Sarah Parcak made one the most exciting discoveries in recent years: she discovered 3,000 ancient settlements around the site of the ancient city of Tanis. In the film *Raiders of the Lost Ark*, Tanis is discovered by the adventurer and archaeologist Indiana Jones. In reality, Tanis is much larger than the lost city in *Raiders*, and Dr Parcak and her team of researchers have uncovered a large system of buried streets and houses. In fact, they have possibly found around 132 new ancient Egyptian sites altogether – some over 5,000 years old. It is no surprise that, since her discovery, Dr Parcak has been called the real Indiana Jones.

The reason Dr Parcak's discovery is so amazing is that none of the sites are visible from the ground. So how did Dr Parcak make such an incredible find? The answer is simple: she used satellites to take infra-red photographs of the Nile valley. The images show what is under the ground. Her team spent a year studying the satellite images and were astonished by the number of sites they found, including over 1,000 tombs and 17 new pyramids around Tanis alone. When a team of excavators was sent to Egypt

they confirmed that there were two pyramids hidden under the desert in Saqqara, the ancient burial site near modern-day Cairo. It was an exciting moment. 'To excavate a pyramid is the dream of every archaeologist,' Dr Parcak told journalists.

The use of satellite technology has been called space-archaeology. Dr Parcak has also used the images to look for new sources of water in Egypt. She is very excited about the future and hopes that more young people will become interested in archaeology. She also hopes to train young Egyptians to explore and dig the sites. 'There is enough to be excavated for 50 generations to come,' she says.

5 Family life

1 Look at the photo. Who do you think the people are? Are they friends or relations?

2 Work in pairs. Which words from the Vocabulary box are used to describe these things?

build	clothes	hair
height	jewellery	skin

3 ⊙ *5.1* Listen to Lee and Reem talking about the people in the photo. Tick words from the vocabulary box. Answer the questions.

1 Who do they finally decide is in the photo?
2 Who does Reem's mother look like?

4 Think of someone in the class. Describe him/her. Can your partner guess the name?

Appearance		
bald	fair	smart
a beard	a headscarf	smiling
a cap	a moustache	thin
dark	a necklace	a watch
earrings	a ring	wavy
elegant	slim	well-built

61

Speaking

1 Work in pairs. Discuss the questions.

  1 Who do you get on with the best in your family? Why?

  2 Is there anybody you don't know well in your family? Why?

Reading and listening

CHECK IT!

2 Read the texts quickly. Which relation is each person talking about?

> a sister cousins grandparents a parent

3 ◎ **5.2** Read and listen to the texts. <u>Underline</u> the adjectives which describe the relations. Put the words into two groups: *appearance* and *personality*.

> ◗ appearance: smart, well-dressed

4 Use some of the adjectives in Exercise 3 to describe people in your family. Write at least five sentences.

> ◗ My parents are easy-going.

1

I love them both. They're really cheerful and they have great stories to tell of when they were young. They're a bit old-fashioned, but they try to keep up with the latest mobile phones and computers, and things. They don't like using them, though. They both had thick, wavy dark hair when they were young, but it's very grey now! When they go out, they always look smart and well-dressed.

Aisha

2

I love going to their house! They're the same age as me and we all get on really well. My aunt is really easy-going and she lets us eat in front of the TV or play computer games in the living room. They're even allowed to play loud music – but only when the neighbours are out. However, she makes them do their homework as soon as they get home from school. I can talk to them about my problems, too. They're really kind and funny and they cheer me up if I'm feeling bad-tempered.

Omar

3

She's tall and slim and quite sporty. She usually wears jeans or a tracksuit, but she looks really elegant in a dress. When we were younger, we shared a bedroom. She was a bit annoying because she was messy and I'm really tidy. Mum wrote a list of rules for us and put it on the bedroom door – you mustn't borrow each other's things, you must tidy up every day, you mustn't eat in the bedroom. That sort of thing. She can sometimes be a bit self-centred, but we get on really well. She still doesn't let me borrow her clothes, though!

Kelly

Working with words: compound adjectives

5 **Look at the examples. Then find more compound adjectives in the text.**

They're a bit old-fashioned.

They always look smart and well-dressed.

 See Working with words, Page 120

Grammar: permission and obligation

6 **Complete the table.**

Permission to do things
I _____ go out with my friends.
We _____ stay out after 10 p.m.
Can you wear earrings at school?

Obligation to do / not to do things
I _____ phone them.
We _____ share a bedroom.
You _____ knock on the door.
You _____ touch my things.
Do you have to go home before 10 p.m.?

No obligation to do things
I don't _____ worry.

The past simple of *must* is *had to*.

 **See Grammar GPS, Page 128**

7 **Read the sentences from the text and choose the correct options.**

1 She lets us eat in front of the TV.

   a We can   **b** We can't   **c** We must

2 They're even allowed to play loud music.

   a They can   **b** They can't   **c** They must

3 She makes them do their homework as soon as they get home from school.

   a They can   **b** They can't   **c** They must

4 She still doesn't let me borrow her clothes, though.

   a I can   **b** I can't   **c** I must

 See Grammar GPS, Page 128

8 **Rewrite the sentences with the words in brackets.**

1 I can't use my sister's mobile phone. (My mum / let)

2 We can't wear jeans at school. (allowed)

3 I can go out with my friends at the weekend. (My parents / let)

4 I have to do my homework before I go out. (My dad / make)

5 Can you invite friends round? (allowed)

Speaking

9 **Look at the pictures. Ask and answer questions with the verbs in the box.**

be allowed to   can   have to   let   make

A: Do you have to wear a uniform at your school?

B: Yes, we do. / No, we don't.

Grammar: reflexive pronouns (*himself*, etc.) and *each other*

10 **Complete the sentences from the texts.**

1 We talk to _____ about everything.

2 She tells really funny stories about _____ when she was my age.

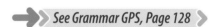 **See Grammar GPS, Page 128**

11 **Complete the sentences with words from the box or *each other*.**

myself   yourself   herself   himself   itself ourselves   yourselves   themselves

1 I looked at _____ in the mirror.

2 The sisters get on well with _____ .

3 We haven't spoken to _____ since Monday.

4 Did you enjoy _____ at the party, Ahmed?

5 Self-centred people only think about _____ .

 If you have time

How many different words do you know for these things? Use a dictionary to help you.

hair colour   hairstyles   eye colour

Listening

1 How much do you know about China? Make notes for two minutes. Then compare with your partner.

2 ⊙ **5.3** Listen to Jin, a Chinese-American student. Does he talk about the things in your notes?

CHECK IT!

3 ⊙ **5.3** Read the questions. Then listen for the answers.

1 What's the population of China?
   a 1 million   **b** 1.3 billion   **c** 3.3 billion

2 How many Chinese people live in cities?
   a 13 per cent   **b** 30 per cent   **c** 70 per cent

3 How long is the Great Wall of China?
   a 400 km   **b** 6,000 km   **c** 6,400 km

4 What colour means good luck to the Chinese?
   a white   **b** red   **c** blue

5 When were the Beijing Olympic Games?
   a 2007   **b** 2008   **c** 2009

Reading and listening

4 Read the text quickly. Who are 'the little emperors'?

STUDY SKILLS

5 ⊙ **5.4** Read and listen to the text. Are the sentences true or false?

1 Chinese families have become smaller since 1979.

2 In Chinese cities, teenage boys play a lot of sports.

3 Chinese families don't have much money to spend on their children.

Speaking

6 Work in pairs. Do you think Chinese families are similar to families in your country? What are the similarities – and the differences?

🏠 HOME | 🐾 ANIMALS | 🌐 **PEOPLE AND PLACES** | 🏃 ACTIVITIES | 🎥 VIDEOS

🌍 PEOPLE AND PLACES
The little emperors

Traditionally, Chinese families had lots of children. Everyone looked up to and obeyed the father. But Chinese families have changed. In 1979, the Chinese government took a decision which had a big impact on society. It was a time when the government was worried about the population increase. Now Chinese families can't have more than one child. Most of the teenagers in the big cities are only children.

Teenagers who have no brothers or sisters can feel lonely. 'If you fall out with your friends, there's nobody else to talk to at home,' says one girl. 'If you have an argument, you have to make things up quickly. If you don't make things up, there is nobody to spend time with. In many cities there are few sports centres or places where

teenagers can get together. Boys spend the evening in internet cafés, instead of socialising. The cafés have broadband connections which are fast and cheap, and addiction to online gaming is a problem.

On the other hand, many of these Chinese teenagers say they feel independent and confident. They don't let other people take decisions for them. Only children get lots of attention from their parents and their grandparents. Each child has six adults looking after them! They get the best food and clothes. Most of them go to extra English classes after school. Parents who have only one child usually have more money to spend on these things.

The children are under pressure because they must do well. Education and success are important in Chinese society. In fact, these only children are called 'little emperors' because now, in Chinese families, they are the people who everybody must obey and respect.

Working with words: phrasal verbs for relationships

7 Look at the examples. Then find five more phrasal verbs in the text.

You can't fall out with your friends.
You have to make things up quickly.

➤➤ *See Working with words, Page 120* ➤

Grammar: relative pronouns and relative clauses

8 Complete the sentences with words from the text.

1 A person who has no brothers or sisters is an ....

2 A time when most people socialise is the ....

3 A place where teenagers play online games is an ....

4 Two things which are important in Chinese society are .... and ....

➤➤ *See Grammar GPS, Page 128* ➤

9 Look at the example. Then ⊙circle⊙ the relative pronouns and <u>underline</u> the relative clauses in the text.

..... a decision ⊙which⊙ <u>had a big impact on society</u>.

> We can use *that* instead of *who* or *which* in the sentences in the text. For example: *... a decision that had a big impact on society.* Note that there is no comma (,).

➤➤ *See Grammar GPS, Page 128* ➤

10 Complete the sentences with *who, which, where* or *when*.

1 An emperor is a man .... rules a country.

2 'Joe's' is a café .... we can meet our friends.

3 The connection .... is the fastest is broadband.

4 The girl .... fell out with her best friend was lonely.

5 The 1970s was a time .... many things changed.

6 The teenagers .... have got the most money are only children.

11 Choose the correct options (a, b or c) to complete the text.

A family tree is a kind of diagram (1) .... explains your family. It shows the relationships (2) .... connect people, for example parents and children. The tree shows (3) .... people were born. There are different spaces (4) .... the people's names are written. Each generation is written on the same line. Your ancestors – the people (5) .... came before you – are at the top of the tree.

	1 a which	**b** who	**c** where
	2 a who	**b** that	**c** when
	3 a that	**b** which	**c** when
	4 a that	**b** where	**c** which
	5 a which	**b** who	**c** when

Speaking

12 Work in pairs. Write + (positive) or – (negative) next to each adjective.

▶ *annoyed* –

> annoyed   anxious   cheerful   confident
> disappointed   embarrassed   excited   lonely
> pleased   upset

13 When do you feel annoyed or anxious? Tell your partner. Give details of the situations. Try to use all the words in the box in Exercise 12. Use these or your own ideas.

> arguments   birthdays   exams   holidays
> mistakes   new people   parties
> sports competitions

A: *I feel anxious before an exam.*
B: *Me too! Especially when I haven't studied.*

Specific information

1 Before you listen to or read a text, read the questions carefully.

2 Decide what kind of information you need to find: a number, a date, a fact, etc.

3 When you listen to or read the text, focus only on finding that information.

Talking about problems

Reading and listening

1 **Look at the photo. Is Reem feeling upset or excited?**

2 🔘 **5.5** **Read and listen to the dialogue. Check your answers to Exercise 1.**

3 **Read the dialogue again. Complete the expressions Jack uses to show interest or surprise.**

   1 I _____ !
   2 Tell _____ _____ _____ _____ .
   3 Go _____ !

Jack: Hey, Reem. What's wrong?

Reem: I've fallen out with Lee!

Jack: I can't believe that. You get on really well.

Reem: Not now!

Jack: Calm down! Tell me about it. What happened?

Reem: Well, you know we were planning to go horse riding in the summer holidays. …

Jack: Yes.

Reem: Well, it's not going to happen!

Jack: Calm down! Tell me all about it. What happened?

Reem: Well, we were studying at my house yesterday evening. He said he wanted to talk about the holidays.

Jack: Go on, what did he say?

Reem: He said he didn't want to go horse riding anymore because his friend has invited him to visit him and his family in the USA this summer.

Jack: Well, that's not so bad! He probably thought it was a good opportunity. I'm sure he didn't want to hurt your feelings.

Reem: I know, but I was really looking forward to learning to ride! Anyway, we argued and he went home without saying goodbye.

Jack: Have you made it up yet?

Reem: No. He hasn't spoken to me all day!

Jack: Look, Reem, it's not the end of the world. He's probably upset at the moment, too. I can talk to him.

Reem: Good idea. He usually listens to you.

Jack: Cheer up! I'm still your friend. And Lauren is, too!

Reem: Yes, I know. Thanks, Jack.

4 🔘 **5.6** **Listen and repeat the *Useful expressions*. Focus on your intonation.**

Useful expressions

What's wrong?
I can't believe that!
Calm down.
Tell me all about it.
Go on! What **did he say**?
That's not so bad.
Cheer up.
It's not the end of the world.

Speaking

5 Work in pairs. Choose one of the situations in the box and write a dialogue. Follow the dialogue map to help you.

> You've fallen out with a friend.
> You've just broken your mum's favourite cup.
> You haven't passed your exams.
> Your best friend is leaving the school.

Student A   **Student B**

1 Ask what's wrong. → Answer A's question.

2 Show surprise/ interest and ask what happened. → Give more information.

3 Say the situation isn't so terrible. → Disagree with A.

4 Cheer your friend up. → Respond to A's comment.

5 Say something positive.

Writing: a description of a person

1 Read Lee's description of his brother. Write the number of the paragraph next to the information.

> his style / clothes   his age and what he does
> his personality   his eyes, hair and skin
> his build

2 Lee mentions the similarities between himself and Cheng. <u>Underline</u> the sentences with *both* and *neither*.

 *See Grammar GPS, Page 129*

3 Rewrite the sentences using the words in brackets.

Cheng and Lee are tall. (Both of)

▶ *Both of them are tall.*

1 Cheng and Lee have got dark hair. (Both of)

2 They have got fair skin. (both)

3 They haven't got blue eyes. (Neither of)

4 They don't buy their clothes in shops. (Neither of)

5 They like the same clothes. (both)

---

6 Take turns. Practise saying the dialogue. Then choose another situation from the box in Exercise 5 and role-play the conversation.

CHECK IT!

7 Read Lee's comments. Choose the best responses.

1 I've fallen out with Reem.
   a What's wrong?
   b I can't believe that!

2 Reem's upset because I'm not going horse riding with her in summer holidays.
   a Good idea.
   b Cheer up! It's not the end of the world.

3 I think she's really angry with me!
   a Go on! What did she say?
   b Tell me all about it.

Pronunciation: homonyms with the sound /eə/

8 🔊 **5.7** Listen to the words in each pair. Is the pronunciation the same (S) or different (D)? Then practise saying the words.

1 cheer	chair		**4** they're	there
2 pair	pear		**5** where	wear
3 their	there		**6** hair	here

9 Practise saying these sentences.

1 There's a chair over there.

2 She's wearing a pair of jeans.

3 Their brother has fair hair.

4 Choose a person in your family and make notes about them. Say how this person is similar to or different from you. Use the information in Exercise 1. Then write a description.

1 My older brother Cheng is 19 and he's studying at university in London. He's really clever and confident. He's always cheerful too. He's friendly and helpful, and he always phones or sends me an email every week.

2 We're quite similar in many ways – we're both tall and slim, and we've both got straight, dark hair. Both of us are fair-skinned because we both take after our mum, who's English. Neither of us has got blue eyes. Cheng's eyes are dark brown, almost black, but mine are just a boring, light-brown colour.

3 I like my brother's style. He usually wears trendy T-shirts and so do I! Neither of us buys our clothes in shops – we always buy them online.

Reading

1 Work in pairs. Look at the photos. What can you see?

2 ⊙ **5.8** Read and listen to the text and <u>underline</u> the following information.

   1 the official languages which are spoken in Canada

   2 places in Canada

   3 nationalities of people who live in Canada

3 Read the text again and answer the questions.

   1 Which areas of Toronto does the writer enjoy visiting, and why?

   2 What can you buy in Kensington Market?

   3 What does the writer like best about his city?

Canada

Culture

Canada today is a multicultural society. We have two official languages, English and French, but many other languages are spoken too. Immigrants from all over the world have come to live here. Each community brings its own customs and traditions, and as a result daily life can be very interesting!

For example, I live in Toronto – the most multicultural city in the world. There are neighbourhoods of people from all over the world. Chinatown and Little India are two of the biggest ethnic communities in the city. I love going there to experience the vibrant sights and sounds, and the delicious smells from all the restaurants and food stalls! There are also large communities of Europeans, as well as Africans, Japanese, South Americans and First Nation people, like me.

My family are Canadian Inuit, from Nunavut in north-west Canada. My parents moved to Toronto before I was born. We live in an area called Kensington Market. It's a great place to live. The streets are lively, and full of shops and street vendors selling ethnic clothes, food and art. Once a month the streets are closed off to traffic for a music festival, where you can enjoy some of the best folk music in Canada.

The people who live here could be from anywhere across the globe. You can hear people speaking many different languages, from German and Russian to Arabic and Taiwanese. However, people quickly learn to communicate with each other in English. I suppose that's what I love most about Toronto – the fact that people from such a variety of languages, cultures and religions manage to live together despite all their differences.

4 Find words in the text which match the definitions.

1 People who go to live in a different country.

2 Things which people do as part of their cultural traditions.

3 Areas of a city where people live.

4 People who sell things in the street.

Listening

5 ⊙ **5.9** Listen to a radio show for young people in Canada. Where is Nunavut?

6 Listen again. Choose the correct answer (a, b or c).

1 Why does Ravi want to know about Nunavut?
  a He has family who live there.
  b He needs the information for his studies.
  c He's going there on holiday.

2 Who lives in Nunavut?
  a People from many different countries.
  b Mostly Inuit people.
  c Inuit, Americans and Canadians.

3 What is the weather like in Nunavut?
  a Freezing cold in winter and very hot in summer.
  b Freezing cold all year.
  c Freezing cold in winter and not very warm in summer.

4 What languages are spoken there?
  a English, Inuktitut and other Inuit languages.
  b English and Inuktitut and American Indian languages.
  c Inuktitut and Inuit languages.

5 How do young people learn about their traditions?
  a They go to classes after school.
  b They read about them at school.
  c They learn about them from older family members.

Project

Has the way of life changed a lot in your country? How were your grandparents' or great-grandparents' lives different to yours? What are the biggest changes? Work in pairs and make a poster.

History and English
The Canadian Inuit

1 Work in pairs. Discuss these questions.

1 What is the traditional diet of the Canadian Inuit?

2 What were their traditional clothes and homes like?

3 How did their lifestyle change after World War II?

4 How did the young people save their culture?

2 Read about the history of the Inuit and check your answers.

●●●

The traditional Inuit lifestyle
The Inuit have lived in the Arctic regions of Canada (Nunavut) for more than 1000 years. They were nomadic and hunted animals such as whales, seals and polar bears. They did not grow food, but ate the berries and plants they could find. Their diet also included fish and seaweed. They travelled across the snow and ice using sleds pulled by dogs. The boats they used for fishing were the original kayaks. Inuit families and communities were large. In winter, they built dome-shaped homes out of the ice, called *iglus*. In the summer they lived in tents made out of animal skins. They also used skins and large bones to make clothes, shoes and knives, as well as small sculptures. Most of these things were shared with other members of the community.

The 1960s to 1999
Before 1940, the Inuit had little contact with other people, but that changed after World War II. North Americans and Europeans built air bases and radar stations. They built towns for the people who came to live and work there. Some Inuit moved to the towns to look for work, and access to health care improved. As a result, the population grew so large that hunters could not provide food for everyone. Many more people abandoned the traditional way of life. During the 1950s and 1960s, the Inuit were forced to move to the towns. Their children had to go away to school in the bigger cities. When they left school, they fought to protect the Inuit culture and their traditional lands. In 1999, the Canadian government created a separate Inuit territory, called Nunavut.

The Inuit today
Although still part of Canada, Nunavut has a lot of independence. The population is almost 100 per cent Inuit, including the local government. They can make many of their own rules and the land belongs to them. They have their own education system, health system, media and businesses. Unfortunately, many Inuit people do not have jobs and are quite poor. Some Inuit still go whale hunting and Inuit arts and crafts are popular.

3 Work in pairs. Do you think the traditional Inuit way of life was better than the modern society they live in today?

Test your skills

Language response

1 Read the sentences. What do you think the missing word is – a noun, a verb or an adjective?

  1 I love my sister. She's funny and _____ .

  2 My dad and I _____ really well. We like the same things.

  3 There are three _____ in my family – two boys and a girl.

2 Read the sentences in Exercise 1 again and write words that can go in each gap.

3 Look at the options for each gap in Exercise 1. Are any of the words that you wrote here? Choose the correct answers.

  1 a kind   **b** kinder   **c** kindest

  2 a fight   **b** take after   **c** get on

  3 a children   **b** child   **c** brothers

CHECK IT!

4 Read the text and choose the correct option (a–c).

> Dear Jenny,
> Thanks for sending the photos of your holidays. You're a (**1**) .... photographer than me! The last time I (**2**) .... a photo, I chopped off everyone's heads! China looks amazing! (**3**) .... the people nice? Everyone looks friendly. When did you get back? Let's meet up at the weekend – school (**4**) .... again on Monday!
> Sara

  1 a good   **b** better   **c** the best

  2 a was taking   **b** take   **c** took

  3 a Was   **b** Did   **c** Were

  4 a starts   **b** was starting   **c** start

Listening

1 Which time is different from the others?

  1 13.00   3 p.m.   three o'clock

  2 half past six   16.30   six thirty

  3 quarter to nine   20.45   9.45

2 Do you know how to say these numbers?

  1 3   13   30   300   3000

  2 5   15   50   500   500,000

  3 9   19   90   900   9,000,000

3 ⊙ **5.10** Listen and circle the correct times and numbers.

  1 13.00   3 p.m.

  2 half past six   16.30

  3 20.45   9.45

  4 13   30

  5 500   500,000

  6 9   9,000,000

CHECK IT!

4 ⊙ **5.11** Listen to the conversation. Which person are they talking about?

  a   **b**   **c**

Punctuation: using colons and dashes

1 Add colons (:) or dashes (–) to these sentences. Add commas where necessary.

1 I think it's a photo of a mum and a dad and their four children two sons and two daughters.

2 It's my favourite class this afternoon double maths.

3 That building over there the really tall one is where my dad works.

4 *Happy Feet* is a great family film it's funny the animation is fantastic and the story is interesting.

5 There are six types of penguin in the Antarctic the Adélie penguin the Chinstrap penguin, Emperor penguins Gentoo penguins Macaroni penguins and Rockhopper penguins.

Grammar: referring back

2 Read the sentences. What do the underlined words refer to?

I'm from northern Alaska. The winters <u>there</u> are very cold. <u>They</u> are also very long. Winter days are extremely short. Although the sun shines most days, <u>it</u> sets very early and rises late. My family moved from Mexico, so <u>we</u> are not used to the climate, especially my mother. <u>She</u> misses the long hot days and warm nights.

1 there: ....

2 They: ....

3 it: ....

4 we: ....

5 She: ....

3 Complete the sentences with *then, there,* or a subject pronoun (*I, you, he, she,* etc).

1 My dad's got lots of wavy, grey hair. ....'s got a moustache, too.

2 The women in my family all look similar. .... are all tall and slim.

3 A hundred years ago, life was very different. There wasn't much traffic ....

4 I love going to my grandparents' house. .... is always peaceful there.

5 The shops in my town are open all day. You can go shopping .... until 10.00 p.m.!

Grammar: word order in defining relative clauses

4 Put the words into the correct order.

1 who / the / Omar Sharif / is / famous / an / actor / became / in /1950s/

2 the / my / where / I / meet / friends / Patty's / is / café /

3 is / welcomes / Canada / country / a / which / immigrants /

4 1980s / was / a / when / the / pop / music / time / changed /

5 people / are / stay / up / night owls / late / that /

Writing practice: a composition

5 Think of a person who you admire. Make notes about this person in your notebook.

Paragraph 1

Who is it? Is it someone famous, a family member, a friend or a teacher? How long have you known him/her?

Paragraph 2

What qualities do you admire about him/her?

6 Organise your ideas for each of the paragraphs above. Then think of a title for your composition.

7 Write your composition. Don't forget to write a topic sentence for each paragraph. Join sentences with a relative clause where possible.

8 Work in pairs. Read your partner's composition and tick (✓) the checklist below.

Has your partner:

- .... used lots of adjectives?
- .... used pronouns correctly?
- .... included a relative clause?
- .... written topic sentences?
- .... written a title?
- .... written an interesting composition?

Spelling: easily confused words

Homophones can cause problems because the words sound the same, but they are spelled differently.

Common homophones

fare	fair	
pair	pear	
right	write	
there	their	they're
wear	where	

Words with similar pronunciation

Words with similar pronunciation can also be easily confused, especially verb forms.

choose	chose (past)
affect	effect
fell (past of fall)	felt (past of feel)
send	sent (You need to hear the final *t* and *d*.)
though	thought

Punctuation

dashes (–) and colons (:)

Colons are used before lists of things or a summary of a list of ideas.

They all wore the same clothes: blue jeans, a T-shirt and trainers. (a list of clothes)

I've a lot of things to do before I go to school: iron my shirt, organise my sports bag, make my sandwiches for lunch and make my bed. (a summary of a list of things to do)

Dashes are similar to colons, but they give more emphasis to the ideas. We use dashes:

before a short summary.

We all went to see the same film – Pirates of the Caribbean! (The emphasis is on the name of the film.)

to join two clauses together.

I suppose that's what I love most about Toronto – the fact that people from such a variety of languages, cultures and religions manage to live together despite all their differences. (The second clause gives the important information.)

Mum wrote a list of rules for us and put it on the bedroom door – you mustn't borrow each other's things, you must tidy up every day, you mustn't eat in the bedroom. (You could use a colon, but this list needs to be given emphasis.)

to interrupt a sentence.

We went to see the film – Pirates of the Caribbean – at the big cinema in the city centre. (You could use commas here but using dashes gives more importance to the name of the film.)

Grammar: subject pronouns for referring back

I	you	he	she	it	we	you	they

Subject pronouns substitute nouns. In a text they refer back to the subject of the previous sentence or paragraph.

I get on well with my sister. We like the same music and have the same hobbies. (We refers back to the people in the first sentence – the speaker (I) and her sister.)

I had a party last week. It was great fun and all my friends came. (It refers back to the party.)

We also use the adverbs *there* and *then* to refer back to place and time. *I don't have classes on Monday afternoon, so we can meet then.* (then = on Monday afternoon)

Nunavut is in Canada. People speak English and Inuktitut there. (there = in Nunavuk, Canada)

Grammar: sentence structure in defining relative clauses

A *A dentist is someone who looks after your teeth.*
A dentist is someone is the main clause in the sentence above. The part in blue is the defining relative clause. It tells us who a dentist is.

B *The hotel where we stayed was lovely.*
In this sentence, *where* is the subject and the relative clause (the part in blue) tells us which hotel was lovely.

Word order

The relative pronoun follows the main clause. It cannot be separated from the subject(s) of the main clause.

In sentence A, *a dentist and someone* are the subjects.

In sentence B, *the hotel* is the subject.

Useful expressions: describing a person

I have known **Max** for **many years / all my life.**
Patricia is a great person. I admire her because **she's intelligent and self-confident.**
One person that I admire is …
I really like/admire **Theo** because …
Jamal is **kind and friendly.** He always listens when **I'm upset / sad.**
Mariam is very **easy-going and open-minded.** She's never **self-centred.**
She is someone who **you can trust / talk to.**
William is always **cheerful,** even though he **has a disability / has had a hard life.**
I like spending time with **Ahmed:** he makes me laugh.

6

Science and technology

GRAMMAR
Learn about the first conditional; predictions with *will/won't*, *may* and *might*; and *going to* for plans and intentions.

SKILLS
Read about the first episode of *Star Trek*, and American sci-fi.

Listen to students' plans for the future, and a discussion about sci-fi books and films.

Write instructions.

COMMUNICATE!
Make offers and requests, and accept help.

VOCABULARY
Learn words for technology, and science subjects.

Work with verbs and prepositions, and phrasal verbs.

Technology	
an e-reader	a microchip
a DVD	a mobile phone
an earpiece	an MP3 player
a flat screen TV	a modem
GPS	a tablet
a laptop	a webcam
a memory stick	

1 Look at the photo and choose the best caption.

   a This high-tech earpiece can send and receive messages and photos.

   b This microchip is smaller than a postage stamp, but it can store more information than 12 CDs.

   c Technologists have designed a hand-held screen which is also a webcam and video camera.

2 ⊙ **6.1** Listen to Lauren and Reem. They have to guess gadgets with five questions. What are the three gadgets? Find them in the Vocabulary box.

3 Work in pairs and prepare a questionnaire to find out who knows the most about technology in your class. Write five questions about things in the Vocabulary box. Use these verbs or your own ideas.

copy files	change settings	download music
install	use	store photos

▶ *Do you know how to copy files on a computer?*

4 Work with a new partner. Ask and answer your questions. Then compare answers with your first partner. Who will you ask for help in future?

Speaking

1 Look at the photo. Which film or TV series are these characters from? How many science-fiction films and TV series can you name? Tell your partner about the ones that you like best.

Reading and listening

2 Read the newspaper article quickly and answer the questions.

   1 When was the article written?

   2 What is it about?

   3 What does the journalist predict?

3 ◉ **6.2** Read and listen to the article. Which *Star Trek* gadgets exist today? What do we call them?

The Daily News Sept 8, 1966

Last night's TV: *Star Trek*

The first episode of a new science-fiction series was shown on NBC last night. *Star Trek* is about a spacecraft which travels faster than the speed of light. The show is based on three ideas about the 22nd century. First, we'll find other life forms in our galaxy. Second, we won't fight with these aliens. And third, we'll have high-tech gadgets which will make amazing things possible.

Let's think about these predictions. If we find life forms on other planets, will they be intelligent? I hope so. But we human beings might not be friendly – I don't think we'll believe in the idea of peace two hundred years from now. But this is science fiction, so we can be optimistic! And *Star Trek*'s idea of life in the future is a lot of fun. For example, we'll be able to talk to each other with hand-held 'communicators'. And we'll be able to have conversations with people who are on different planets, on a giant TV screen. You won't have to use a pen and paper to write because you'll have an electronic notepad. And if you get ill, the doctor won't have to examine you – a machine will 'read' your body. The strangest machine consists of a 'teleport' which will transport people to a different place in a second!

The ideas are very entertaining, and in my opinion there's only one problem with *Star Trek*: the acting. The TV company will have to get better actors. If they do that, the show might be a success. If the acting doesn't improve, *Star Trek* won't last for more than one series. Of course, my prediction may be wrong. I can't see into the future!

Grammar: first conditional

4 Complete the table with the words in the box.

get   find   will   won't

Condition	Result
If you _____ ill,	a machine will read your body.
If the acting doesn't improve,	*Star Trek* _____ last for more than one series.
If we _____ other life forms,	_____ they be intelligent?

 The future form of *can* is *will be able to*. The future form of *must* is *will have to*.

➡ **See Grammar GPS, Page 129**

5 Choose the correct option.

   1 We *don't need / won't need* bookshops if digital books *become / will become* popular.

   2 If you *go / will go* online, you *find / will find* the information you want.

   3 *Can you / Will you be able to* email me if you *don't take / won't take* your computer?

   4 If we *want / will want* to see them on the computer, we *have to / will have to* get a webcam.

   5 How *do you contact / will you contact* me if you *haven't got / won't have* a mobile?

6 Complete the sentences with the verbs. Remember to use the present simple after *if*.

1 If Sally _____ (not / phone), we _____ (not / know) where she is.

2 _____ it _____ (be) quicker if she _____ (send) a text message?

3 Andy _____ (not / get lost) if he _____ (use) the GPS.

4 I think my mum _____ (buy) me an MP3 player if I _____ (pass) my exams.

5 _____ I _____ (can save) my new settings if I _____ (change) them?

Grammar: predicting

7 Match the sentences (1–5) with the meanings (a–c).

1 We will find other life forms.
2 We might find other life forms.
3 We won't find other life forms.
4 If other life forms exist, we will find them.
5 We may find other life forms.

a The prediction is not 100 per cent sure.
b The prediction is 100 per cent sure.
c The prediction depends on a condition.

 May and *might* have the same meaning and the same form for *I, you, he, she, it, we* and *they*.

 See Grammar GPS, Page 129

8 Look at the text again and find predictions to match each meaning (a–c) in Exercise 7. Compare with your partner.

9 Complete the predictions. Use *will, won't, may* or *might* depending on your opinion. Compare with your partner.

1 Faster-than-light travel _____ possible. (be)
2 We _____ life on other planets. (find)
3 We _____ teleporters instead of cars. (use)
4 We _____ on space stations in the Earth's orbit. (be able to live)

Speaking

10 Work in pairs. Write at least two questions for each picture.

▶ *Do you think we'll find aliens?*
What do you think they will look like?

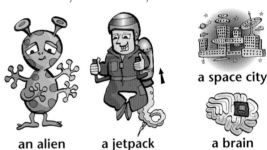

an alien   a jetpack   a brain
a space city

11 Work with a new partner. Ask and answer the questions.

A: *What do you think aliens will look like?*
B: *I (don't) think they'll have … / They might have …*

 We use *I (don't) think …* + *will* to express opinions. We don't use *I think* + *won't …* .

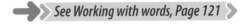 See Grammar GPS, Page 129

Working with words: verb + preposition

12 Look at the examples. Then find verbs with the prepositions *on, in, to* and *for* in the text.

Let's think about these predictions.
It consists of a 'teleport'.

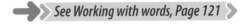 See Working with words, Page 121

 If you have time
How quickly can you complete the words? They are all related to technology.

| ear……… | hand-……… | high-……… | lap……… |
| micro……… | note……… | web……… | |

Speaking

1 Work in pairs and discuss the questions. Use words from the Vocabulary box.

1 Which science subjects do you study at school?

2 Which subjects are the most difficult?

3 Which subjects are the most interesting?

4 Which sciences help us understand our world?

5 Which sciences will help us to live better in the future?

> astronomy   biochemistry   bio-technology
> botany   chemistry   ecology   genetics
> geography   geology   physics   psychology
> zoology

Reading and listening

2 🔘 **6.3** Read and listen to the text. Do you think the stories are true or false?

STUDY SKILLS

3 Read the text again. Are the words in red nouns, verbs or adjectives?

4 Read the sentences with the red words in story 1 and choose the correct meanings.

physicians
a things which scientists use
b doctors

wireless
a without wires
b made of wire

5 Work in pairs and guess the meanings of the words in red in the other stories.

Working with words: phrasal verbs

6 Find these verbs in stories 1 and 4. Choose the correct meaning.

turn up the volume = **a** increase, **b** decrease

come back to Earth = **a** leave, **b** return

➡️ **See Working with words, Page 121** ⟩

Science fact or fiction?

1 A team of engineers, computer scientists and physicians is working on a 'mind-reading' system. They have put a microchip into a man's brain. The microchip is connected to a computer. The man can switch on his email just by thinking about it. He can also turn up the volume of his TV. Now the team is going to make a smaller, wireless version of the system, which is called BrainGate.

2 Japanese schoolchildren love their robot teacher, Saya. She can speak, smile and tell students off. The Japanese government is going to invest millions of dollars in robot research and says it's going to put a robot in every Japanese home by 2015. However, psychologists predict that robot teachers won't take over from humans because they will never be able to inspire their students.

3 British geneticists are going to vaccinate all school children with a 'smart gene'. The team of university scientists has identified the gene for intelligence on human DNA. Now they are going to put this gene into children under the age of twelve. Professor R. Ubbish says the vaccination won't work on adolescents or on children who don't like science.

4 Biologists are going to study the effects of space travel on microscopic life forms. They want to find out if it's possible to survive for long periods in space. The micro-organisms are on an unmanned spacecraft which set off for Mars in 2009. It will land there, pick up some Martian soil and then come back to Earth. A team of geologists is going to analyse the soil. If everything goes well, the spacecraft will get back to Earth in two years' time.

Grammar: *going to* for plans and intentions

7 Look at the example below. Find six more plans or intentions in the text.

The team is going to make a smaller, wireless version.

 **See Grammar GPS, Page 129**

8 Complete the plans (a–e) with *going to*. Then match them with the situations (1–5).

a Scientists _____ the temperature of the ice. (measure)

b It _____ the medicine next year. (sell)

c They _____ here next year. (come back)

d Astronomers _____ signals in outer space. (look for)

e The government _____ more universities. (build)

1 A new telescope started working today.

2 The Arctic ice gives us information about climate change.

3 A company is developing a new cure for flu.

4 Lots of students want to study for a degree.

5 The scientists didn't have time to explore all the forest.

9 Work in pairs. Read the comments from school students. What do you think they are *going to* or *not going to* do? Write sentences with the verbs in brackets.

1 'I'm good at biology at school.' (She / be)

2 'Chemistry is my favourite subject.' (He / work)

3 'Everyone in my family is a scientist.' (He / study)

4 'I finish school this year.' (She / look for)

5 'I'm doing French and English at school.' (He / visit)

Listening

CHECK IT!

10 ◉ **6.4** Listen to three students talking about their plans for the future. Match the sentences (a–d) with the students (1–3). There is one extra sentence.

a He/She is going to study geology.

b He/She wants to be a zoologist.

c He/She is going to live abroad.

d He/She isn't going to follow the family tradition.

11 ◉ **6.4** Listen again. Complete the sentences.

1 Student 1 knows all about _____ .

2 Student 2 isn't interested in _____ .

3 Student 3 is good at _____ .

Speaking

12 Write questions with the words and *going to*. Think about your own answers. Then work in pairs. Ask and answer the questions. Ask follow-up questions.

1 What / do / this afternoon?

2 What / watch / on TV tonight?

3 Who / get together with / this weekend?

4 What / do / in the next holidays?

5 What / do / on your next birthday?

STUDY SKILLS

Difficult words

1 Decide if the word is a noun, a verb or an adjective.

2 Read the sentence carefully. Look at the words before and after the difficult word. What word can you use instead of this word?

3 If you can't understand the sentence without understanding the word, use a dictionary.

6C Offering, requesting and accepting help

Reading and listening

1 🔊 **6.5** Read and listen to the dialogue. What does Lauren want to buy? Does she decide to buy one?

2 Read the dialogue again. Lauren asks for help three times. What does she say? Which expression is more formal?

3 Look at the *Useful expressions*. Write C for customer or A for assistant next to each expression.

🔍 We use *Shall I* to make offers.

➡️ **See Grammar GPS, Page 129**

4 🔊 **6.6** Listen and check your answers to Exercise 3. Listen and repeat.

Useful expressions

How can I help you?
I'd like to **look at some mobile phones**, please.
I'll **show you our selection**.
Thank you very much.
Can you **explain how it works**?
Yes, of course.
Shall I **find some cheaper models**?
Yes, please.
Could you **show me something more basic**?
I'll **take it!**

Assistant:	How can I help you?
Lauren:	I'd like to look at some mobile phones, please.
Assistant:	If you follow me, I'll show you our selection.
Lauren:	Thank you very much.
Assistant:	These models are all very popular at the moment.
Lauren:	I really like this one. It doesn't look like a phone! Can you explain how it works?
Assistant:	Yes, of course. You switch it on here …
Lauren:	Oh, yes … Reem, can you hold my bag for me?
Reem:	Sure.
Lauren:	Great, thanks. OK, has this phone got an MP3 player and a camera?
Assistant:	Yes, it has. I'll put in a battery, just a moment.
Reem:	Lauren, have you seen the price? It's expensive.
Lauren:	I know. I'll have to check with my mum. I don't think she'll let me spend that much!
Assistant:	Well, with this model you can download large files and send emails.
Lauren:	Hmm … I don't think I'll need all that.
Assistant:	Shall I find some cheaper models?
Lauren:	Yes, please. Could you show me something more basic?
Assistant:	That's no problem. I'll just put this back in the box … . Now, what about these?
Lauren:	Oh, I like this one.
Reem:	Yeah, me too. It's just like mine!
Lauren:	OK! I'll take it!

CHECK IT!

5 Choose the correct option (a, b or c) for each situation.

1 You are in a shop. You want to ask the shop assistant for help. What do you say?

  a I'll help you.

  b Can I help you?

  c Could you help me?

2 The shop assistant offers to show you some cameras. What does he say?

  a Can you show me this camera?

  b I'll show you our cameras.

  c How can I help you?

3 You want the shop assistant to show you a phone. What do you say?

  a Could I show you this phone?

  b Shall I show you a different model?

  c I'd like to see this phone, please.

4 The shop assistant offers to show you how a camera works. How do you respond?

  a I'll take it!

  b Thank you very much.

  c Yes, of course!

6 Work in pairs. For each situation, offer or request help, and respond. Take turns.

1 carry / bags

2 put in / paper

3 fix / bike   **4** connect / webcam

Pronunciation: connected speech

7 🔘 *6.7* Listen to the sentences. Notice how the underlined words are linked. Listen and repeat.

1 Here are the headphones. Put <u>them on</u>.

2 I'd like to <u>look at</u> it.

3 Switch <u>it on</u>.

4 Put <u>it in</u> the printer.

5 <u>Turn up</u> the volume.

Writing: giving instructions

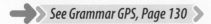

1 Read the emails. What does Jack want? Does Reem help?

2 Find examples of *so that* and *in order to* in the email. Then complete the sentences with *so that* or *in order to.*

1 I bought a DVD player .... we can watch films at home.

2 Reem bought an MP3 player .... listen to music.

3 We installed Skype .... we can make free phone calls.

4 My dad wants GPS .... drive to my cousin's new house.

➤➤ *See Grammar GPS, Page 130* ➤

3 Rewrite the sentences in Exercise 2 with the other expression.

4 Write a message to your partner asking for help. Reply to your partner's message and give instructions. Use these or your own ideas.

> download photos from a camera onto a computer
> put phone numbers into a phone memory
> record a TV programme

⬤⬤⬤

Reem,
Can you explain how to put music files on my MP3 player? Could you come round tonight and help me? See you later!
Jack

⬤⬤⬤

Hi Jack,
Sorry – I'd love to help, but we're going to my grandparents' tonight. Shall I come round tomorrow? If you want to try it by yourself, this is what you do:

1 Download the songs that you want onto your computer.

2 Save the songs in a folder so that they are easy to find.

3 Plug in your USB cable in order to connect your MP3 player to the computer.

4 Click on 'My computer' so that you can open your MP3 player.

5 Drag your music files onto your MP3 player.

Reem

Reading

1 **Look at the photos. Which of these things can you see?**

> aliens   planets   machines   the moon   robots   UFOs

2 *6.8* **Read about American sci-fi. How many American authors can you find?**

3 **Read the text again and answer the questions.**

1 When did science-fiction writing become popular?
2 Where was science fiction first published?
3 What was the problem with Robert A. Heinlein's first book?
4 Which author's books help us to understand our society?
5 Which author's stories were often made into films?

USA.

Culture

Science fiction – or sci-fi – is a different way of looking at the world. It became popular at a time when electricity, machines and new forms of transport were changing people's lives. European writers like Jules Verne and H.G. Wells wrote new stories for the new times – science fiction.

In the early 20th century, sci-fi stories in magazines and comics sold millions of copies in the USA. Books by American writers like Ray Bradbury, Robert A. Heinlein, Ursula K. Le Guin and Philip K. Dick are translated into almost every language in the world.

Some writers, such as Robert A. Heinlein, focused on the kind of future that technology might bring. Sometimes, that future seemed too incredible. Heinlein's first book was rejected by some publishers. They said that 'to reach the moon' wasn't believable!

Other authors, such as Ursula K. Le Guin, wrote about culture and identity in the future. Le Guin was born in 1929 and wrote her first story when she was 11 years old. Her stories are often about contact between alien worlds in a way that teaches us something about our own human culture and society.

Both Heinlein and Le Guin influenced other writers, but neither of them had the impact on American films that Philip K. Dick had. *Blade Runner*, *Total Recall* and *Minority Report* are just three of the films which were adapted from Philip K. Dick's stories. Most of his stories are about space and time, parallel worlds and genetic engineering. He describes a future that is cruel, dangerous and frightening. Perfect for Hollywood movies!

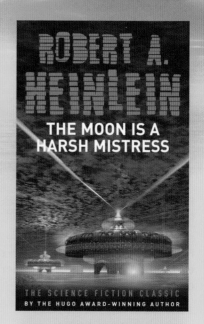

THE MOON IS A HARSH MISTRESS

THE SCIENCE FICTION CLASSIC
BY THE HUGO AWARD-WINNING AUTHOR

4 Work in pairs. Find the words in the text and try to guess their meaning. Then use the words in the sentences.

way   incredible   reach   impact

1 The spacecraft set off two years ago and will _____ Mars next year.

2 The experiment didn't work, so they will try a new _____ of doing it.

3 The meteor made a huge _____ when it hit the Earth.

4 Astronauts have walked on the moon. I think that's _____ .

Listening

5 ⊙ *6.9* Listen to two people talking about science fiction. Choose the correct option (a–c).

a They both think films are better than books.

b They agree that books are better than films.

c They can't agree which are better – films or books.

6 ⊙ *6.9* Listen again. Complete the sentences with *man* or *woman*.

1 The _____ 's favourite actor is Tom Cruise.

2 The _____ doesn't like Philip K. Dick's stories.

3 The _____ 's favourite film was *E.T.*

4 The _____ thinks the book *War of the Worlds* is old-fashioned.

5 The _____ recommends the film *Minority Report*.

Project ▸▸ What is your favourite science-fiction film or story? Write a paragraph saying who directed/wrote it and what it is about. Then write a second paragraph saying why you like this film or story.

Physics and English

Light and telescopes

1 What do we use to look at the planets? Read about telescopes and find out how they work.

How do we see things?

Light travels in straight lines. When light hits an object, it reflects off the object and comes back into our eyes. For example, light travels out from the sun in all directions. When the light reaches a planet, it is reflected back by the planet. From Earth, we see this light and so we see the image of the planet. The rest of space looks black because there are no planets to stop the light and reflect it back to us.

How do telescopes make things seem larger and closer? Telescopes collect the straight lines of light (A) and change their direction. They do this with a lens (B). The lens bends the light so that it focuses to a point (C). This makes it easier to see, but the image is still very small. In order to see the image, we have to make it bigger. A second lens is used to do this (D). In this way, when the reflected light reaches our eyes (E), the objects seem larger and closer than they are.

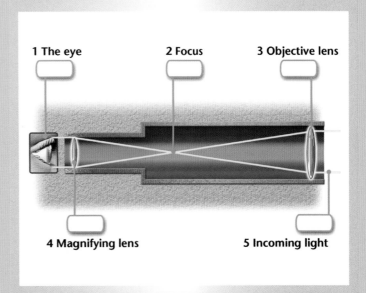

1 The eye   2 Focus   3 Objective lens

4 Magnifying lens   5 Incoming light

2 Complete the diagram with the letters (A–E) from the text.

Listening

HOW TO...

identify the main idea of a text
- Read the task instruction and the options. Identify the overall topic.
- For matching questions, read the questions again and underline the key words.
- For multiple-choice questions, try to predict words you will hear.
- The first time you listen, choose the correct answer. The second time, check your answers.

Important! Be careful with words that have similar meanings.

1 Read the task instruction and options. Circle the overall topic and underline the key words.

You will hear three people talk about their favourite gadgets. Match the statements (a–d) with each speaker (1–3). There is one extra statement.

a It's really useful when I'm travelling.

b I like it because I can listen to music everywhere.

c It makes it easy for me to stay in touch with my parents.

d It's easy to use and the picture is great.

2 Read the task instruction and options. Write words you think you will hear for each option.

You will hear someone talk about their favourite gadget. What is the gadget?

a a webcam

b a memory stick

c a mobile phone

3 6.10 Now listen and do the task in Exercise 1.

CHECK IT!

4 6.11 You will hear someone talk about a birthday present. What is the present? Choose the correct option (a–c).

a a laptop

b an MP3 player

c GPS

Reading

HOW TO...

understand the organisation of a text
- Identify the first and last sentences.
- Write the correct sequence for the other sentences. Linking words can help you.
- If there are options, compare your sequence with them. Check that the other options are incorrect. Be careful when you compare your sequence with the options.

1 Put these linking words into logical sequences.

1 then   first   in the end   next

2 finally   also   secondly   firstly

2 Find the first and last sentences in a note about using a camera. Then put all of the instructions in the correct sequence.

a First put the battery into the camera.
b That's how easy it is!
c Here are the instructions for my camera.
d Finally, save or delete your picture.
e Press the button to take your picture.
f Then switch on the camera.

1	2	3	4	5	6

3 Match your sequence with the correct option (a–c).

a c, a, f, b, e, d   **c** c, a, f, e, d, b

b a, f, e, d, c, b

CHECK IT!

4 Put the sentences in a logical order. Choose the correct option (a–c).

a Click on 'OK' to save the photos to your folder.
b And that's it! Good luck!
c First, connect the camera and your computer with the cable.
d Here are the instructions for saving the photos from my camera.
e Choose the folder where you want to put the pictures, for example 'My photos'.
f With the cable connected, switch on the camera.

a d, f, a, b, e, c   **c** c, d, f, e, a, b

b d, c, f, e, a, b

Spelling: words with /k/ sounds

1 Add the letters *c, k* or *ck* to complete the words. Use the *Writing bank* to help you.

1 Can you predi _____ t who will win the next World Cup?

2 I fell off my bicy _____ le yesterday!

3 He's going to study geneti _____ s at university.

4 Listen! I can hear someone kno _____ ing on the door.

5 The teacher hasn't finished mar _____ ing our exam papers yet.

6 We need to conta _____ t the university about a place next year.

7 National Geographic magazines have some very interesting arti _____ les.

8 There's a clo _____ on the wall in our classroom.

9 I love science fi _____ tion films.

10 MP3 player have be _____ ome very popular.

Punctuation: apostrophes

2 Rewrite the sentences using contracted forms. Add apostrophes (') where necessary.

1 Kevin is good at science so he will probably study physics at university.

2 Science fiction writers became very popular during the 1950s.

3 Arthur C. Clarke and Douglas Adams novels have influenced many other science-fiction writers work.

4 A: Our class is going to the National Space Centre with Mr Browns class.

B: That will be fun. I would like to go there one day, too.

Grammar: *in order to, so,* and *so that*

3 Answer the questions. Use the words in brackets and add any other words.

1 Why did you buy those walking boots? (so that / go trekking)

I bought them _____

2 Why does Penny sit at the front of the class? (so / see the board)

She sits there _____

3 Why has Saimma left school early? (in order to / doctor's)

She's left early _____

4 Why are you cleaning the kitchen? (so / Mum / have a rest / this weekend)

We're doing it _____

5 Why does your brother do his homework at lunchtimes? (so that / not have to do / evenings)

He does it _____

Writing practice: talking about plans (in a letter)

A friend is coming to stay with you for a few days and has sent you this email.

Hi (your name),

Thanks for inviting me to stay with your family next week. I'd love to come! However, I'm not sure about the best way to get there. Shall I come by train or by bus? What do you think?

Also, where is the best place to meet when I arrive?

What are we going to do while I'm with you? Are there any interesting places to visit? As you know, I love sport and science.

I'm really looking forward to seeing you all. Give my love to your family.

Write soon,

(your friend's name)

4 Make notes about the following points in your notebook. For each of your ideas give reasons and explanations.

- The best way to get to your town/city
- The best place to meet
- Interesting places to visit
- Things to do

5 Now write an email to your friend. Use purpose clauses where possible: *in order to, so/so that*. Use the *Grammar GPS* on page 129 to help you.

6 Work in pairs. Read your partner's letter and imagine you are the friend who receives it. Write *yes* or *no* next to the questions below.

Do you know the best way to get to your friend's house and why?

Do you know where to meet and why?

Do you know which places you can visit?

Has your friend suggested things to do?

Do you know why your friend has suggested these activities?

Has your friend ended the letter in a friendly way?

Spelling: words with /k/ and /ks/ sounds

Use the rules below to help you understand spelling. Try to learn the correct spellings and refer to this section for help.

Words with the /k/ sound
Words spelled with k, ck or ch

Words are spelled with the letter *k* if the sound /k/ is followed by *e, i,* or *y.*
brake   like   risky   ski   spoken
The letter *k* is also is used at the end of a word with one syllable, and can follow any sound: break check luck milk soak

Words spelled with ck

ck is used at the end of a word with one syllable and follows a short vowel:
knock   clock   black   stick
A few words are spelled with *ch* and make a /k/ sound:
chemistry   schedule   scheme   school   technology

Note: other words beginning *ch* make a /tʃ/ sound:

chair   cheese   change

Nouns ending in ction

The *c* makes a /k/ sound. The /k/ sound followed by *tion,* is pronounced /kʃən/:
direction   fiction

Adjectives ending ic

The *c* makes a /k/ sound.
economic   electronic   microscopic   optimistic

Nouns ending in cs

Irregular singular nouns ending in *cs* are pronounced /ks/.
physics   economics   gymnastics

Words spelled with c and cc

The letters *c* or *cc* make a /k/ sound. Most other words are spelled with a single letter *c* to make the /k/ sound:
cycling   contact   consist   difficult
direct   obstacle   microphone   webcam
Sometimes the letter *c* is doubled:
accommodation   account   occupy   soccer
Words with the letter *a, o, u* + the sound /ks/ are usually followed by double *c*:
accept   accident   accent   success

Words with the /kw/ sound

These words are always spelled with *qu* to make the /kw/ sound:
acquire   enquire   queen   quiet   require   request

Words with the /ks/ sound: The letter x

Words beginning with the letter *e* + *x* make the sound /ks/:
expect   explain   extra   excellent   explore
Words with the letter *a, o, u* + the sound /ks/ are usually followed by double *c*:
accept   accident   accent   access
eccentric   success   vaccination

Words ending with /æks/, /eks/, /ɪks/ and /ɒks/

box   complex   fox   prefix   suffix   relax

Words ending in the /kst/ sound

There are a few words that end /kst/.
next   text
The past forms of a few regular verbs end with the sound /kst/.
faxed   mixed   taxed

Punctuation: apostrophes

Contracted forms

We use an apostrophe (') with contracted forms of auxiliary and some modal verbs. The apostrophe shows where letters have been removed:

am = 'm   are = 're   had/would = 'd   have = 've
is /has = 's   shall/will = 'll

We do not use contracted forms:

when the word is at the beginning of a question.
Shall I open the window?

after plural nouns with are.
The girls are going out.

in positive short answers.
Yes, I will. Yes, we have.

with decades.
the 1960s, the 1990s

with abbreviations which use capital letters.
six DVDs

Possession

We use an apostrophe to show possession:
before the possessive s with singular nouns:
Mohammed's bag

after the possessive s with plural nouns:
the boys' coats

Note: With two names, we use an apostrophe after the second name if the people possess the same item:
James and Sarah's house.

Names ending in *s* are usually written *s's* but it is also correct not to write the final *s*:
James's coat or *James' coat*

Grammar: *in order to, so,* and *so that*

We use ***in order to, so,*** and ***so that*** to talk about why we do an action. We call them 'purpose clauses'.

Useful expressions: letters and emails

Making plans and suggestions
I think it's best if you take the train because it's quicker.
If you arrive early, I will meet you at the station.
I think you should come on the bus so that I can meet you at the bus stop near my house.
We can go to the cinema in the evening, if you like.

Beginning and ending your email/letter
Thanks/Thank you for inviting me to stay.
I'd love to come to your house next weekend.
I'm (really) looking forward to hearing from you.
Say hello to everyone.
Write soon.

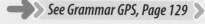
See Grammar GPS, Page 129

Grammar consolidation
Prepositions → See Grammar GPS, Page 130

Prepositions after verbs

Some verbs can be followed by prepositions: *consist of, believe in.* Some verbs are never followed by prepositions.

1 Choose the correct option.

1 Do you listen *the radio / to the radio* every day?

2 My friend apologised *me / to me* after our argument.

3 I usually phone my *grandparents / to my grandparents* on Saturdays.

4 Can you explain *me / to me* how this phone works?

5 Will you call *me / to me* tonight, please? I'll be at home.

6 Read the sentences and discuss *them / about them.*

2 Write the missing prepositions.

1 Who are you talking _____?

2 What are you talking _____?

3 What kind of music do you listen _____?

4 What are you looking _____?

5 Who are you waiting _____?

6 Who are you going shopping _____?

Prepositions in time expressions

3 Complete the sentences with *at* or *on*. Write – if the sentence is already correct.

1 I'm going to visit my friend _____ next month.

2 What are you doing _____ New Year?

3 Where did you go _____ last week?

4 Do you want to meet _____ Saturday morning?

5 I don't like going out _____ night.

6 We watched a great TV programme on TV _____ last night.

Prepositions in phrasal verbs

4 Match the prepositions with opposite meanings.

back	from	in	into	on	up
down	forward	off	out	out of	to

5 Complete the sentences with prepositions from Exercise 4.

1 Where do you come _____?

2 What time did we set _____?

3 Can you fill _____ this form, please?

4 I'm not making _____ with him!

5 Calm _____. It's not important.

6 I'll call you _____!

Prepositions that are easy to confuse

6 Choose the correct option.

1 Can you translate this *in / into* your language?

2 How many students are *in / into* your class?

3 I opened the door and the cat ran *in / into* the garden.

4 There are lots of animals *in / into* the park.

5 The book was made *in / into* a film.

7 Which preposition can be used to complete all these sentences?

1 Ben fell _____ his bike.

2 Joshua got _____ the bus.

3 Sara took the picture _____ the wall.

4 Robert took _____ his coat.

Vocabulary

1 Complete the sentences.

The man's got dark (1) s_____ .
He's also got a (2) b_____ and
a (3) m_____ . He hasn't got
a lot of hair. In fact, he's quite (4)_____ .
He's wearing a (5) w_____ on his wrist.

1 mark per item: …/5 marks

2 Choose the correct adjectives.

1 My friends have moved away. I'm *lonely /
excited*.

2 I feel *anxious / annoyed* at the dentist's.

3 I was *pleased / upset* after I argued with my friend.

4 I feel *embarrassed / cheerful* on sunny days.

5 I was *disappointed / confident* when I got a D
for my project.

1 mark per item: …/5 marks

3 Write the names of the objects.

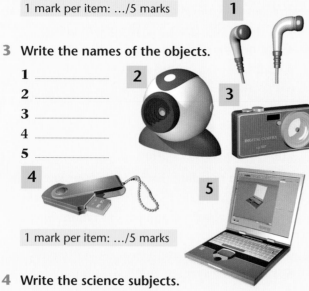

1 _____
2 _____
3 _____
4 _____
5 _____

1 mark per item: …/5 marks

4 Write the science subjects.

1 the study of space and the
planets _____

2 the study of soil and rocks _____

3 the study of animals _____

4 the study of the brain and
behaviour _____

5 the study of DNA and genes _____

1 mark per item: …/5 marks

5 Complete the sentences.

1 People who are not modern are _____ .

2 My brother's going _____ with his best
friend tonight.

3 I don't believe _____ aliens.

4 Can you pay _____ my bus ticket?

5 How did you find _____ my name?

1 mark per item: …/5 marks

Grammar

6 Rewrite the sentences with the words in brackets.

1 We can't wear trainers at school. (allowed)

2 My mum makes me tidy my room. (have to)

3 I can't stay up late. (my parents / not let)

4 Can you stay out after ten o'clock? (allowed)

5 Mobiles are not allowed in class. (must / use)

1 mark per item: …/5 marks

7 Complete the sentences with one or two words.

1 You're self-centred. You only think about
_____ .

2 My cousin's in the USA. We see _____
in the summer holidays.

3 My brothers never fight with _____ .

4 Did he cut _____ when he fell?

5 We enjoyed _____ at the party.

1 mark per item: …/5 marks

**8 Complete the sentences with *who, when, which*
or *where*.**

1 The rocket _____ went to Mars has landed.

2 A person _____ writes books is an author.

3 The time _____ people sleep is the night.

4 The man _____ wrote *I, Robot* was Russian.

5 The café _____ we had lunch was great.

1 mark per item: …/5 marks

9 Make first conditional sentences.

1 If you _____ (take) your mobile, I
_____ (call) you.

2 My dad _____ (worry) if I _____
(not / phone) home soon.

3 If there _____ (be) life on other planets,
_____ it _____ (be) friendly?

4 If we _____ (not / use) the GPS, we
_____ (not / find) the road.

5 _____ Ben _____ (listen) to me if
I _____ (talk) to him?

1 mark per item: …/5 marks

**10 Complete the sentences with the correct form
of *will be able to* or *will have to*.**

1 (I can) _____ download files.

2 (We must) _____ arrive on time.

3 (Can I) _____ watch TV this evening?

4 (We can't) _____ send photos.

5 (Must I) _____ save this file?

1 mark per item: …/5 marks

Communicate!

11 Choose the correct response (a–c).

1 This phone seems very complicated.
 a Thank you very much.
 b Shall I find a simpler model?
 c How can I help you?

2 Do you want to borrow my camera?
 a Could you show me something more basic?
 b I'd like to look at some cameras.
 c Thanks. Can you explain how it works?

3 This memory stick costs £5.
 a Shall I find some cheaper models?
 b I'll take it.
 c Yes, please.

4 How can I help you?
 a I'll show you our selection.
 b I'd like to look at some laptops.
 c Shall I show you how it works?

5 Can you switch the printer on?
 a Yes, please.
 b Yes, of course.
 c I'd like to switch the printer on.

2 marks per item: …/10 marks

12 Do the pairs of words sound the same (S) or different (D)?

1 pair	pear	
2 their	there	
3 cheer	chair	
4 hair	here	
5 where	were	

2 marks per item: …/10 marks

13 Complete the sentences with *so that* or *in order to*.

1 I borrowed a mobile .... make a phone call.

2 I'm going to study medicine .... I can become a doctor.

3 We went on the internet .... we could find the information.

4 My friend lent me his bike .... I didn't have to walk to school.

5 We got broadband .... have a faster connection.

2 marks per item: …/10 marks

14 Complete the dialogue with the expressions.

> Cheer up. Let's go shopping!
> I can't believe that!
> It's not the end of the world.
> Tell me all about it.
> What's wrong?

Lisa: **(1)** ....

Jo: I'm worried about my IT test results.

Lisa: **(2)** ....

Jo: I did badly and my dad always gets angry when I get bad marks.

Lisa: **(3)** .... Isn't he easy-going?

Jo: Not really. This is a disaster!

Lisa: **(4)** ....

Jo: I know. But you don't know my dad.

Lisa: **(5)** ....

2 marks per item: …/10 marks

15 Complete the text with these words.

after	all	both	both of	going to	neither
that	them	where	will		

> There are five people in my family. I've got two sisters. I take **(1)** .... my dad. **(2)** .... us are tall and dark. **(3)** .... of my sisters is dark, in fact they are very blonde. My parents are **(4)** .... scientists and we **(5)** .... like sci-fi. Next month, we're **(6)** .... take part in a *Star Trek* convention. It's a big party **(7)** .... *Star Trek* fans meet. My sisters love dressing up. Both of **(8)** .... are going to the convention as aliens **(9)** .... have invaded Earth! I think we **(10)** .... have a great time.

1 mark per item: …/10 marks

Total: …/100

I can...

Tick (✔) what you can do.

	★★★★★	★★★	★
I can talk about problems.			
I can make offers and requests.			
I can accept help.			

True story: the scientist and the film-maker

The poem, the *Rubaiyat of Omar Khayyám*, is known all over the world and it has been translated into many languages. Several films have been made about the life of its author, Omar Khayyám. The most recent film, *The Keeper*, was released in 2005 and was directed by Iranian-American Kayvan Mashayekh.

The story is told through the eyes of 12 year-old Kamran, an Iranian-American growing up in Texas. His older brother, Nader, is dying. Nader is *the keeper* of their family history and he begins to tell Kamran the true story of their ancestor, Omar Khayyám. Tragically, Nader dies before he finishes the story. If Kamran wants to know the rest of the story, he will have to fly to Iran to hear it from his elderly grandfather, who is on his death bed.

So why did the director choose to make a film about Omar Khayyam? Mashayekh says he wanted to make a film about pride, dignity and the need to keep stories from the past alive. And if you want to help young Persians to learn about their cultural heritage, you won't find a better story than Khayyám's. Khayyám was born in Samarkand (now part of the Republic of Uzbekistan) in the 11th Century and was taught by Imam Muaffak. When the Imam was called to work for Sultan Malik Shah I, he brought Omar to the court as his adviser. It was here that Omar Khayyám made important discoveries in mathematics and astronomy. He was famous for his work on problems in algebra and geometry, which were later used by European mathematicians.

As an astronomer, Khayyám helped to build a fantastic observatory for the Sultan, Ulugh Beg, who was also a mathematician and astronomer. From this observatory, he studied the Earth's orbit around the sun and made many tables showing his findings. He then invented a new calendar, called the Jalali calendar, which became the official Persian calendar. Khayyám's calculations were very accurate and the Jalali calendar became the basis for the modern Iranian calendar.

The Keeper is certainly a beautiful film. But will Mashayekh achieve his ambition? Anyone who goes to see the film will certainly learn about Persian history, astronomy and poetry. It may even teach young people the importance of their own family histories.

Omar Khayyám

Old Samarkand

1 **Work in pairs. Look at the photos. What can you see?**

2 **Read the text quickly. Who is the scientist and who is the film maker?**

3 **Read the text again and write the names.**

   1 Who lives in Texas and who lives in Iran?

   2 Who are the keepers of the family history?

   3 Who travels to Iran?

   4 Who wants to teach young people to feel proud of their culture?

   5 Who brought Omar Khayyám to the sultan's court?

   6 Who wanted a new observatory?

   7 Who uses Khayyám's astronomical calculations for their calendar?

   8 Who will learn about Persian history?

4 **Find words and expressions in the text which match the definitions.**

   1 used to describe someone who is going to die soon

   2 knowledge, buildings and customs which are passed down through the generations

   3 the circle which a planet travels in around a star

   4 used to describe something which is correct and precise

5 **Work in groups. Imagine that you are a film-maker. You want to make a film to teach people about your cultural heritage. Who will you choose to make the film about? Why?**

7

Good Citizens

GRAMMAR

Learn about reporting verbs: *ask, invite, order, remind, tell, want* and *warn*; reported requests and orders; and indirect questions.

SKILLS

Read about some young heroes, the Global Citizen Corps, and a Maori tradition in New Zealand.

Listen to a conversation at a conference, and an interview with a Maori girl.

Write a note with personal news.

COMMUNICATE!

Give and take messages.

VOCABULARY

Learn words for cities and towns, and good citizens.

Work with words that are easy to confuse, and irregular nouns.

Cities and towns	
a city centre	pollution
art galleries	public
football	transport
pitches	shopping
gyms	centres
ice rinks	sports
leisure centres	stadiums
litter	a temple
a mosque	traffic
office blocks	youth centres

1 Where do you think the photo was taken? Give reasons.

2 Tick the things in the Vocabulary box which are in your city or town. Add three more things.

3 ⊙ *7.1* Listen to three people talking about where they live. Answer the questions for each person.

  1 Do they live in the city or in the country?

  2 Do they like living there?

4 Work in groups of four. Which is better – living in the city or in the country? Use words from the Vocabulary box and these expressions.

There are more … / There aren't as many … /
It isn't as … / It's less … in the city/country.

Speaking

1 Work in pairs. Discuss these questions. Use the vocabulary from the box to help you.

  1 What makes a good citizen?

  2 How does somebody become a hero?

considerate	polite
kind	respect the law
tolerant	save lives
honest	show courage
helpful	be respectful
look after the environment	a volunteer

Reading and listening

2 Read the texts quickly. Match the photos (a–c) with the texts (1–3).

a

b

c

Teen Heroes

1 Connor Rowntree

In 2009, British teenager Connor Rowntree was playing with an aerosol can and a lighter when it exploded. The 15-year-old was upstairs at a friend's house when the accident happened. Connor's body caught fire and he jumped out of the window onto the grass outside. His friend threw water over him to put out the flames. As they waited for the ambulance, Connor's older sister, Leanne, tried to keep him calm. He had 90 per cent burns and little chance of survival. The brave teenager had to have almost 100 operations and spent 14 months in hospital. Connor is an inspiring young person who has used his experiences to help others. With the help of the local Fire and Rescue Service, he started a campaign to warn young people not to play with fire, and to remind them to be careful with fireworks. He says he wants to be a firefighter when he leaves college. Connor won the *BBC Teen Hero* award in 2010. A year later, the *Wellchild* charity invited him to meet Prince Harry and to receive the *Bravest Young Person Award*.

2 Jayme Saunders

In 2011, Canadian teenager Jayme Saunders was riding a dirt bike with her school friend, David Weismiller. They were going across a bridge when they lost control and hit rocks in the shallow water below. Jayme broke her leg, but David's injuries were more serious. He had broken several bones and damaged his lung and an artery. Luckily, Jayme knew First Aid. She calmly put her leg in a splint, using a branch and wet clothes. Then the selfless teenager stayed in the cold water for several hours looking after David. Eventually a driver saw them and called an ambulance. As Jayme watched the paramedics at work, she asked them to explain what they were doing and decided she wanted to be a paramedic, too. Both David and Jayme recovered from their injuries. Jayme was later awarded the silver medal for bravery from the National Lifesaving Society.

3 Gaurav Singh Saini from India won the National Bravery Award in 2010 for saving more than 60 lives in a crush at the hillside temple of Naina Devi. 13 year-old Gaurav clearly remembers that rainy day in 2008. He was at the temple with his parents when they heard people shouting 'Landslide!' In fact, there was no landslide but people panicked and started running down the steep narrow paths that led to the temple. Barriers collapsed and people fell on top of one another. Gaurav started looking around to see how he could help other people. Then he saw a wire which was hanging between two food stalls. He jumped up and got hold of the wire and swung over the people below. He told a young boy to hold onto his leg and pulled him up. When they saw this, other people wanted him to help them, too. Courageous Gaurav pulled more people onto the wire. They then pulled themselves along the wire to a roof, and to safety. 'I am proud that I could save so many lives,' says heroic Gaurav.

3 ⊙ **7.2** Read and listen to the stories. <u>Underline</u> the adjectives which describe the young heroes.

4 Read and listen again. Who do you think said these things? Write a letter (a, b, c, d or e) next to each comment (1–6).

  1 'Don't play with fire!'

  2 'Don't forget to be careful with fireworks.'

  3 'Do you want to come to the ceremony?'

  4 'Can you explain what you're doing, please?'

  5 'Hold on to the wire!'

  6 'Help me!'

  a People at Naina Devi temple

  b Gaurav

  c Jayme

  d The organisers at Wellchild

  e Connor

Grammar: reporting verbs

5 Look at the text again and complete the table with the reporting verbs below.

want	remind	ask	warn	tell	invite

a Connor	....	young people	not to play with fire.
b He	....	them	to be careful with fireworks.
c The charity	....	him	to meet Prince Harry.
d She	....	them	to explain what they were doing.
e He	....	a boy	to hold onto his leg.
f They	....	him	to help them.

➡️ *See Grammar GPS, Page 131* ➤

6 Match the direct speech in Exercise 4 (1–6) with the reported statements (a–f) in Exercise 5.

1 .... **2** .... **3** .... **4** .... **5** .... **6** ....

7 Read the sentences below. What did the people in red actually say? Choose the correct option.

1 The boy wanted to help the old man.
   a 'Can you help me, please?'
   b 'Can I help you?'
2 The old man asked the boy to take him across the road.
   a 'Take me across the road now.'
   b 'Can you take me across the road, please.'
3 The boy told the old man to be careful of the traffic.
   a 'Can you be careful of the traffic?'
   b 'Be careful of the traffic.'
4 The old man reminded the boy to use the pedestrian crossing.
   a 'Don't forget to use the pedestrian crossing.'
   b 'Do you want to use the pedestrian crossing?'
5 The boy warned the old man not to cross the road on his own.
   a 'Don't cross the road on your own.'
   b 'Do you want to cross the road on your own?'

8 Report each person's words with the verbs.

➤ 'Go home, everybody!' (tell / everybody)
She told everybody to go home.

1 'Don't move.' (Jayme / warn / David)
2 'Please phone for an ambulance.' (Jayme / ask / the driver)
3 'Keep calm!' (Leanne / tell / Connor)
4 'Don't panic!' (fire chief / order / the crowd)
5 'I'd like you to help me.' (David / want / firefighters)

CHECK IT!

9 Look at the notices (a–d) and complete the sentences (1–4).

a REMEMBER! SHOUTING IS NOT ALLOWED.

c NO LITTER. USE THE BINS.

b Please Wait For Assistance.

d THIS WATER IS NOT SAFE FOR DRINKING.

1 Sign .... warns people not to ....
2 Sign .... asks customers to .... for help.
3 Sign .... reminds people not to ....
4 Sign .... tells people to ....

Working with words: easily confused words

10 Look at the examples. Which verb is followed by an object pronoun?

say *He said something to my assistant.*
tell *She told me to lock the front door.*

➡️ *See Working with words, Page 122* ➤

If you have time
What can you do to help in these situations?
- A building is on fire.
- A boy has fallen into the river.
- A child is lost in the city centre.
- An elderly lady has fallen over in the street.
- Someone is injured in a road accident.

Speaking

1 Work in pairs. Which of these things are you interested in?

> art   film   going out with friends
> making new friends   music
> people in other countries   sport   the environment

Reading and listening

CHECK IT!

2 Read texts 1–3 quickly. Match each text with the best description. There are two extra descriptions.

a The writer is giving information.

b The writer is asking for advice.

c The writer is inviting someone to do something

d The writer is asking for information.

e The writer is offering advice.

STUDY SKILLS

3 🔘 **7.3** Read and listen to the texts. <u>Underline</u> words with similar meanings to these words.

> hobbies   meeting   take part in
> topics   chance   enjoying yourself
> guitar player   play with

4 What can you remember? Close your book and test your partner. Are the sentences true or false?

1 Bashir's free time activities are water-polo and playing the piano.

2 High-school students can take part in the GCC youth gathering.

3 Bashir will be able to practise English at the GCC gathering.

4 The GCC is a group for people who are interested in making their communities better.

5 Sumaya is one of the organisers of the youth gathering.

Working with words: irregular nouns

5 Look at the examples. Do you know any more irregular nouns?

maths   *Maths is an interesting subject.*

the family   *The family are at home today.*

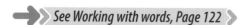

See Working with words, Page 122

Meet Bashir Khoury

1

It's July 2012 and Bashir Khoury, aged 16, from Lebanon is looking forward to the summer holidays. He'll be able to play water-polo with his team, and he might be able to do some acting, which is another one of his interests. But this summer is also Bashir's first time at the Global Citizen Corps international youth gathering, which is in Doha, Qatar this year.

Bashir talks about the GCC youth gathering

'Well, the GCC youth gathering brings together young people aged from 16 to 25, who are interested in improving the communities they live in. They come from all over the world including the Middle East, Europe, Asia, South America and the USA. Everyone who takes part has shown that they have excellent leadership and communication skills. There is a programme of activities based on important global topics – the environment and education are the ones that interest me the most. At the gathering in Qatar, I'll learn how to use film, photography and even sport to help people in my community back home. It's a real opportunity to make a difference. There'll be lots of cultural activities, too. We'll learn about each other's customs and traditions – and we'll do it all in English!'

2 Bashir says ...

'Come and join the Global Citizen Corps and get involved in one of many different projects. You can volunteer to teach in Ecuador, rebuild homes that were destroyed in the earthquake in Haiti or find a project in your local community. Visit our website, where you can read about us and share ideas and experiences. It's not only about helping others, it's also about developing yourself as a person and having fun.'

3

Global Citizen Corps 2012 Guestbook

Date	02-03-12
From	Mohammad Al Fakhri
Subject	application

Hello!

Could anyone tell me how I apply to be a participant at the GCC youth gathering? Also, do you know what the dates of the programmes are?

●●●

Date	10-05-12
From	Sumaya Annan
Subject	closing dinner

Hi there!

I'm attending the youth gathering in Qatar and I'd like to take part in one of the concerts. I sing traditional songs but I need a guitarist or 'oud player to accompany me. Can you tell me if there are any participants who can join me?

Grammar: word order in indirect questions

6 Complete the questions from the text.

Could anyone tell me how .... to be a participant?

Do you know what the dates of the programme .... ?

Can you tell me if .... any participants who can join me?

 See Grammar GPS, Page 131

7 Look at the example. Then rewrite the questions in Exercise 6 without the words in red.

Can you tell me what time it is?

🖋 *What time is it?*

8 Rewrite the questions as polite questions.

1 What day does the youth gathering begin?

2 How do I get to the university from the airport?

3 Will there be time to visit the city?

Listening

9 Look at the groups of words. Which one is the odd one out?

1 laptop   mobile   phone

2 enjoy yourself   feel lonely   have a great time

3 half an hour   a moment   30 minutes

4 book   programme   show

5 photo   picture   signature

CHECK IT!

10 ⊙ **7.4** Listen to two participants at the GCC youth gathering in Doha. Are the sentences true or false?

1 Yasmina saw Nathalie's photo on the GCC website.

2 Nathalie can't remember everyone's names.

3 Nathalie's next session starts in 30 minutes.

Speaking

11 Work in pairs. Plan a party or a school festival. Make notes on time, place, number of people, activities, entry fee, etc.

12 Work with a new partner. Ask and answer questions about the events. Use polite questions.

A: *Can you tell me what your event is?*

B: *Yes, it's an end-of-term party.*

STUDY SKILLS

Synonyms

1 Texts use similar words or synonyms to avoid repetition.

2 When you are answering questions about a text, listen and look for words which are similar to the words in the questions.

3 Write groups of similar words in your notebook.

Reading and listening

1 **7.5** **Read and listen to the dialogue. Are the sentences true or false?**

1 Reem can't go to the picnic.
2 Jack's got a jacket for Lee.
3 Lee's going to take chocolate cookies to the picnic.

2 **Read the dialogue again.** <u>Underline</u> **Jack's message and how Lee's gran passes on the information.**

Gran: Hello.

Jack: Hi. Can I speak to Lee, please?

Gran: Oh, Lee's gone shopping. This is his gran speaking.

Jack: Oh, hello. It's Jack. Could you give him a message, please?

Gran: With pleasure, Jack.

Jack: Can you tell him Reem's going to the picnic tomorrow?

Gran: Yes, of course.

Jack: And remind him to take some biscuits and cake to the picnic. Oh, and can you ask him to lend me a jacket?

Gran: OK. I'll tell him.

Jack: Thank you very much.

Gran: You're welcome.

Later that day

Gran: Hello, Lee.

Lee: Hi, Gran.

Gran: Your friend Jack phoned. Reem's going to the picnic tomorrow.

Lee: Really? That's great!

Gran: He wants to borrow a jacket from you.

Lee: That's OK. I've got two.

Gran: And he asked me to remind you to take some biscuits and cake.

Lee: Oh no, I forgot to buy biscuits at the shops!

Gran: I'll make some chocolate cookies, then. Is that OK?

Lee: Yes, that's great! I'll do the washing up for you! Thanks, Gran.

Gran: Not at all. I'm always happy to help my grandson!

3 **7.6** **Listen and repeat the *Useful expressions*. Focus on your intonation.**

Useful expressions

Could you give **him** a message, please?
With pleasure.
Can you tell him **Reem's going to the picnic tomorrow**?
Remind him to **take some biscuits and cake**.
Can you ask him to **lend me a jacket**?
I'll tell him.
You're welcome.
He asked me to remind you **to take some biscuits and cake**.

CHECK IT!

4 ○ **7.7** Listen to the messages (1–3) and choose the correct answers (a, b or c).

1 What does Jack ask Lauren's mum to do?
   a give a note to Lauren
   b remind Lauren to come to the picnic
   c remind Lauren to bring her camera

2 Why does Lauren phone Reem?
   a to apologise for not meeting her
   b to invite her to lunch
   c to change the time of their meeting

3 What does Reem want Lee to do?
   a phone her back
   b finish their project
   c meet after school today

CHECK IT!

5 Match the questions (1–3) with the answers (a–d). There is one extra answer.

1 Can you give Reem a message, please?
2 What's the message?
3 Can you tell her to phone me back?

a Can you remind her to bring a laptop?
b It's really important.
c Of course. I'll tell her to call you.
d With pleasure.

Writing: personal news

1 Read Lauren's note to her cousin Erin in Ireland. Tick the subjects Lauren talks about.

| her friends | taking part in a competition | | |
| doing sport | Reem and Lee | her family | Jack |

2 Underline these words and expressions in the note. Then choose the correct option.

| Actually | Unfortunately | By the way |
| Guess what? | luckily | Anyway |

> Hi Randa,
> (**1**) *Guess what? / Anyway*, I did my driving test last week. (**2**) *Unfortunately, / Luckily,* I didn't pass. (**3**) *By the way, / Actually,* I was terrible! (**4**) *Anyway, / Unfortunately,* I can try again next month!
> Love, Rosie

3 Write a note to a friend giving them some personal news. Use some of the expressions from Exercise 2.

Speaking

6 You are going to a party with your friend tomorrow. You leave a message with her/his dad. Write the message using these words. Then work in pairs. Take turns to give and take your messages.

> Can you tell her/him … ?
> Remind her/him … .
> Can you ask her/him … ?

7 Work with a new partner. Give the message from Exercise 6 to your partner. Take turns.

Pronunciation: words ending in /p/ and /b/, /k/ and /g/, /f/ and /v/

8 ○ **7.8** Listen and repeat the groups of words.

1	cap	hip	hop	lip	shop	map
2	cab	Bob	sob	rub	job	web
3	back	dock	lock	quick	Jack	lick
4	bag	dog	log	dig	jag	big
5	leaf	life	off	stuff	half	laugh
6	leave	live	of	five	have	drive

9 ○ **7.9** Listen and repeat. Be careful with the final sound.

1	cap	cab	**4**	leaf	leave
2	back	bag	**5**	off	of
3	lick	big	**6**	half	have

> Hi Erin,
>
> Congratulations! You've passed your driving test! (My dad told me!) That's great.
>
> Sorry I haven't written for a while. I've been really busy with the hockey team and rowing club. Actually, I rowed in my first competition race last weekend. Unfortunately, we didn't win, but we didn't come last, either!
>
> How's the tennis? Have you won any competitions this year? By the way, Jack's really good now. He might beat you this year!
>
> Guess what? Lee is going to the USA to stay with one of his friends this summer. Reem was a bit upset about it at first because they planned to go horse riding together. They had a big argument about it. Luckily, they're friends again now.
>
> Anyway, I must go and help Mum with the dinner. Say hello to everyone.
>
> Love,
>
> Lauren

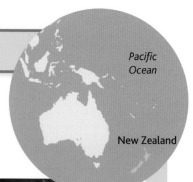

Culture

Pacific Ocean

New Zealand

The Maoris were the first inhabitants of New Zealand and they have ancient and respected traditions. They live in large, extended families. Each family belongs to a tribe, called a *hapū*. Tribes which share ancestors belong to an even larger tribe, called an *iwi*. Even though they may live many miles apart, it is very important for members of the same tribe to have a place to meet – including young people.

In traditional Maori villages there was a large space in the centre, called a *Marae*. This was where the Maoris held important events such as weddings, funerals and traditional celebrations. It was also the place where they met to discuss family issues and to choose their leaders – tribal elders who have a lot of knowledge about the tribe and their traditions.

Today, the Marae is still very important. There is usually a large open space, a meeting house and a dining room. The tribal elders of the Marae are respected and they teach young people about Maori traditions. They also decide when to hold a community meeting. At these meetings, each person is seen as an individual and as a member of the tribe. Everyone has the chance to speak and they work towards agreements that will benefit the whole community.

Nowadays, the idea of family and community is still very strong. Maoris who live in isolated areas will travel miles to their Marae so that they can socialise with their tribe and take part in cultural and spiritual activities.

Reading

1 **Work in pairs. Read the sentences. Are they true for your country?**

1 People live in large, extended families.

2 Young people show a lot of respect for their elders.

3 Large family meetings are held to discuss important issues.

2 ⊙ *7.10* **Read and listen to the text and decide if the sentences in Exercise 1 are true for New Zealand.**

3 **Read the text again and find out:**

1 who the Maori people are.

2 what happens at a Marae.

3 what the results of a community meeting are.

4 **Find words in the text that have similar meanings to the underlined words.**

1 We met <u>the people who live</u> in the town.

2 It's a <u>very old</u> system.

3 Do you have any <u>problems or important topics</u> you want to talk about?

4 The <u>older people</u> of the family are very important.

5 Doing sport will <u>be good</u> for your health.

5 **Work in groups of four. Do you think the Marae is a good idea? Why?/Why not?**

Listening

6 🔘 **7.11 Listen to an interview with Maori teenager, Meri Te Kanawa. Choose the correct answers (a, b or c).**

1 Maori teenagers:
  a a are interested in folk music.
  b are similar to other teenagers.
  c do a lot of sport.

2 *Whanau* means:
  a family.
  b friends.
  c neighbours.

3 *Pakeha* means:
  a Maori teenagers.
  b European New Zealanders.
  c aunts and uncles.

4 The *Marae* in Meri's town:
  a has lots of rooms.
  b has one large room.
  c has a large open space.

5 Visitors to the *Marae*:
  a learn to sing traditional Maori songs.
  b are not allowed to join in the celebrations.
  c are given a special welcome.

Project ▷▷
Work in groups. Write a questionnaire of three to six questions to find out what activities people do in your community or at school to help others, and what projects they have at the moment. Write a paragraph about the results of your questionnaire.

Social science and English

Citizenship: helping others

1 Work in pairs. How many charities or non-governmental organisations (NGOs) can you name? What do they do?

2 Read about the Prince's Trust and answer the questions.

  1 Who does the Prince's Trust help?
  2 How does it help them?
  3 Why is it called the Prince's Trust?

Prince's Trust

The Prince's Trust

About the Trust

The Prince's Trust is a youth charity that helps change young lives.

It gives practical and financial support, developing key workplace skills such as confidence and motivation. The Trust works with 14 to 30-year-olds who have struggled at school, have no families, have not had a job for a long time, or have been in trouble with the law.

It has helped more than 575,000 young people since 1976 and supports 100 more each working day. More than three in four of the young people the Trust helped last year moved into work, education or training.

Around one in five young people in the UK are not in work, education or training. Youth unemployment costs the UK economy £10 million a day in lost productivity.

The Trust's history

The Prince's Trust was started in 1976 by the Prince of Wales. After he completed his duty in the Royal Navy, Prince Charles became dedicated to improving the lives of disadvantaged young people in the UK and began the Trust to carry out this work.

3 Are there any charities similar to the Prince's Trust in your country? What do they do?

Reading

1 **Read the task. Write at least one expression for each function (a–c).**

Read Dan's email. Why has he written to James?
a to apologise for something
b to ask for help
c to give him advice

2 **Write expressions for these functions.**

1 asking for advice
2 making a suggestion
3 agreeing with somebody

3 **Read the email. <u>Underline</u> the functional expressions. Then do the task in Exercise 1.**

Hi James,
Do you remember the Saturday job I told you about? I'm going to apply for it. The application form is complicated. Could you help me with it? You're good at this kind of thing. Can I come to your house at the weekend?
Dan

CHECK IT!

4 **Match the notes (1–2) with the writers' purpose (a–c). There is one extra purpose.**

1 Hi Dan,
No problem, I'm happy to help. Why don't you come round on Saturday morning? See you then.
James

2 Hi James,
I'm glad you enjoyed the film last night. Me too. And you're right, it's a great idea to go and see it again!
Lisa

a to make a suggestion
b to ask for advice
c to agree with somebody

Language response

1 **Read the questions. Where are the speakers?**

1 What time does the show start?
   a at a theatre   b at a conference
2 How much is this camera?
   a at a friend's house   b in a shop
3 Can I leave a message, please?
   a on the phone   b in a classroom

2 **Write at least one possible response to each question in Exercise 1.**

3 **Choose the best answers for the questions in Exercise 1.**

1 a On Saturday evening.   b At 9 p.m.
2 a It's £95.   b I'll take it.
3 a Would you like to   b Certainly.
     leave a message?

CHECK IT!

4 **Match the questions (1–5) with the responses (a–f). There is one extra response.**

1 How far is it to your school?
2 How do I get to the shopping centre from here?
3 Would you like to come with me?
4 What size shoes do you take?
5 How many people live in your neighbourhood?

a Turn left at the end of this street.
b Yes, please.
c Not very many.
d Six months.
e I think I'm an eight.
f It's about two kilometres from here.

Spelling: words with the /z/ sound

1 **Complete the words with the missing letters:** *s*, *z* or *zz*.

1 cou___in
2 free___ing
3 pi___a
4 qui___
5 tho___e
6 gallerie___
7 Japane___e
8 pri___e
9 rea___on
10 vi___it

Punctuation: direct speech

2 **Rewrite the sentences with correct punctuation. Add question marks (?), quotation marks (' '), commas (,) and full stops (.).**

1 Can I speak to Lee please asked Jack

2 Sorry he's not in said Lee's grandmother

3 Could you give him a message please Jack asked Lee's grandmother

4 Of course I can she replied

5 Can you tell him the match has been cancelled said Jack

Grammar: word order in sentences with direct speech

3 **Write the dialogue. Put the words into the correct order. Then add quotation marks, full stops and commas.**

1 asked / Reem / you / are / going / ice-skating / ? /

2 yes / are / we / replied / I /

3 I / me / come / too / can / she / asked / ? /

4 you / course / can / of / told / her / I /

5 come / Great! / round / I'll / house / to / your / said / she /

Writing practice: a narrative

4 **Put the sentences in order to write the beginning of a story.**

___ Many of them were abandoned and it was very quiet.

___ I was going home from school when my mobile rang.

___ 'Can't you download a film?' I asked.

___ I was in a narrow street with old buildings on either side.

___ It was my brother.

___ 'Hi, it's me. Can you get a DVD for the weekend?' he said.

___ 'OK. I'll go to the shop now. What films do you want?' I asked him.

___ 'Anything science-fiction. Phone me when you're in the shop.' he told me.

_1_ It was about four o'clock.

___ When he hung up, I realised I didn't know where I was.

___ 'No, the internet connection's not working properly,' he replied.

5 **In your notebook, organise the beginning of the story in Exercise 4 into sections: paragraph 1, the beginning of the story, then the dialogue, and what happened next in paragraph 2.**

6 **Continue the story in Exercise 5. Write notes for these ideas.**

- What does the writer do next?
- Who does he meet?
- What do they say to each other?
- What happens next?

7 **Now add your ideas to the story. Continue paragraph 2, write your dialogue, and then write about what happens next. Look at the** *Useful expressions* **in the** *Writing bank*. **Check your punctuation carefully!**

8 **Work in pairs. Read your partner's story. Is it interesting? Can you follow the dialogue easily?**

Spelling: words with the /z/ sound

Use the rules below to help you work out why a word is spelled in a certain way. Try to learn the correct spellings and then refer to this section when you need help.

Words which are pronounced with a voiced /z/ are usually spelled with a single letter *s* or a single *z*.

Single letter *s*

Plural nouns after a voiced consonant or after a vowel sound:
fires   hobbies   guitars   days   gyms   hours
burns   lives   situations stadiums neighbours

Verbs ending in s after a voiced consonant or after a vowel sound:
enjoys   has   reminds   shows   saves   warns

Words ending in *es* and *ies* when pronounced /iz/:
changes   communities   hurries   injuries

Many words with a single *s* between two vowels* (or a vowel and *y*):
cheese   Chinese   choose   disease   easy   musems
nose   noise   present result   these   surprise

*Note: crisis is an exception to this rule.
See the /s/ sound in Unit 8. Some words are spelled with *s + e*.

Single letter *z*

Not many words are spelled with the letter *z*. Here are the most common:

Words beginning or ending with *z*
zoo   zero   zebra   zinc   zone   zoom   quiz

Words where the letter *z* is between vowels
prize   size   dozen   freeze
frozen   lizard ozone

Double letter *z* (*zz*)

Only a few words are spelled with double *z*:
blizzard   fizzy   dizzy
jazz   pizza   puzzle

Punctuation: quotation marks

When we write down exactly what someone says, the words are written between opening (') and closing (') quotation marks.

'Can you help me?'

'Don't forget to buy some bread.'

If you want to mention who said the words, you use a reporting verb (say, tell, ask, etc.). For statements, you need to change the full stop before the closing quotation mark to a comma.

'The shops are closed now,' said John.

For questions, you do not use a comma, but remember to use a question mark instead.

'Can you help me?' asked the girl.

Grammar: structure of sentences with direct speech

When you use a reporting verb after direct speech, the subject usually comes before the verb:

'That's a nice jacket,' she said.

'Can I borrow your pen?' Mike asked.

You can also put the verb before a subject which is a noun (<u>not</u> a pronoun):

'Are you hungry?' asked Mum.

The verb *tell* is always followed by an object and *tell* always comes after the subject.

'Put your things away now!' the teacher told us.

You can also write an object after the verb *ask*:

'Can I borrow your pen?' Mike asked Hannah.

Start the dialogue on a new line, a few spaces in from the left margin. Each time the speaker changes, start on a new line.

'Are you hungry?' Mum asked.

'Yes, we're all starving,' everyone replied.

Useful expressions: writing dialogue

Don't write long sentences for each speaker.
If you use a question, follow it with an answer.

Making dialogue sound natural
Use expressions like:
OK.
Oh!
Mmm... ,
Of course, ...

Use different reporting verbs:
ask   order   promise   say   shout   tell   warn etc.
to make your dialogue more interesting and dramatic.
'Help!' shouted the boy.
'Be careful! The floor's wet,' she warned.

Travel

GRAMMAR
Learn about the second conditional, and quantifiers *very, really, quite, a bit, a lot, much* + adjectives.

SKILLS
Read and do a quiz about survival, read about maps, and the Caribbean: a tourist paradise.

Listen to conversations about travel, and holidays.

Write an email with holiday tips.

COMMUNICATE!
Offering help, requesting information, giving advice, making suggestions and giving instructions.

VOCABULARY
Learn words for holidays, holiday packing, and transport.

Work with adjectives and adverbs of manner, and verb + noun combinations.

Holidays

adventure	foreign
beach	hotel
camping	package
cruise	safari
day trip	sightseeing
diving	theme park
family	trekking

1 Work in pairs. Imagine you are the people in the photo. Write your conversation.

2 Work in pairs. What are the best types of holiday for these people? Use ideas from the Vocabulary box.

families with young children	groups of teenagers
people aged 18–30	retired couples
school groups	young couples

3 8.1 Listen to a customer at a travel agency. In the Vocabulary box, tick the holidays the travel agent suggests. Which holiday do you think is best for this customer?

4 What kinds of holiday have you been on? What holidays would you like to go on? Tell your partner.

Speaking

1 Choose a holiday from the list on page 101. What are you going to take with you? Choose things from the box. Then work in pairs and compare with your partner.

> a compass   a first aid kit   a guidebook
> a map   a penknife   a phrasebook
> a rucksack   a sleeping bag   a suitcase
> sun cream   a swimsuit   swimming trunks
> a tent   a torch   a water bottle   waterproofs
> a snorkel   sunglasses   wetsuit

2 Look at the other things in the box. Think of situations where they are useful. Compare with your partner.

Reading and listening

3 ⊙ *8.2* Read and listen to the text. <u>Underline</u> three words which you don't understand. Work with other students to decide the meaning of the words.

4 Work in pairs and do the quiz. Compare your results.

EXPLORER JOURNEYS

Imagine going on a dream trip. Which of these comments sounds like you?

A   'I like having fun. I would go to a beach and a theme park with my friends.'

B   'I love danger and excitement. I would visit places nobody has ever been to.'

C   'I like being comfortable. I would go on a cruise or to a luxury hotel.'

Did you choose B? Perhaps you'd make a good National Geographic explorer. What do you think? Would you be cool in tough situations? Try our quiz and find out how well you'd survive a trip 'into the wild'.

Quiz questions

1 Where would you be if this was the view from your tent?
  a   I'd be in the Sahara desert.
  b   I'd be on a beach in Scotland.

2 What would you do if you found a tarantula in your sleeping bag?
  a   I'd calmly take a photo of it.
  b   I'd scream loudly.

3 Would you panic if you saw this in the water next to you?
  a   Yes, I would! It's a box jellyfish, which is very dangerous!
  b   No, I wouldn't. Jellyfish are harmless.

4 If you got lost at night up a mountain, what would you do?
  a   I'd wait patiently for sunrise.
  b   I'd try to get back to base quickly.

5 If you were on an expedition to find the North Pole, which things would be the most useful?
  a   A map of the stars, a tent and a first aid kit.
  b   A guidebook, a swimsuit and a suitcase.

How did you do?

Mostly 'a's:
You did well! You're knowledgeable and cool-headed. You'd make a good explorer.

Mostly 'b's:
You like travelling dangerously! If the jellyfish didn't sting you, you'd probably have an accident running around mountains in the dark. Luckily, this is only a quiz! Make sure you travel safely in your everyday life.

Working with words: adjective ▸ adverb

5 Look at the examples. Then find six more adverbs of manner in the text and the answer key.

loud   *I'd scream* loudly.

good   *You did* well.

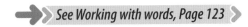 **See Working with words, Page 123**

Grammar: second conditional

6 Look at the introduction to the quiz and complete the table.

Imaginary situation	If I was on a dream holiday,
Action	I .... to a beach.
	I .... places nobody has ever been to.

See Grammar GPS, Page 131

7 Look at the table. Which tense do we use in the part of the sentence with *if* – the present simple or the past simple?

8 Read the quiz questions and complete the table.

Would you panic if you .... this in the water?	Yes, I .... No, I ....
What .... you .... if you found a tarantula?	I'd scream.

 With pronouns, we often use the abbreviation *'d* for *would*: *I'd go, You'd go, He'd go, She'd go,* etc.

See Grammar GPS, Page 131

9 What would you do if you were on a trip abroad? Complete the sentences with the verbs.

1 If I .... (feel) travel sick, I .... (take) a tablet.

2 I .... (buy) a phrasebook if I .... (not / speak) the local language.

3 I .... (not / panic) if I .... (get) lost.

4 If I .... (miss) my train, I .... (wait) for the next one.

5 If I .... (lose) my passport, I .... (go) to the police.

Speaking

10 Write questions with the sentences in Exercise 9. Think of an answer for each question. Use a dictionary to help you.

▸ *What would you do if you felt travel sick?*

11 Work in pairs. Ask and answer your questions from Exercise 10.

A: *What would you do if you felt travel sick?*

B: *I'd go to sleep.*

CHECK IT!

12 Read the advice from an experienced explorer. Write the verbs in the correct forms.

If I was on a trip to somewhere new, **(1 I / not take)** .... any unnecessary risks. You should always plan carefully for the local conditions. For example, if **(2 I / be)** .... in the Arctic, **(3 I / wear)** .... special clothes because you can get frostbite very easily. If **(4 we / go)** .... to an area we didn't know well, **(5 we / ask)** .... local people about possible dangers. It's common sense. Even here in Europe, **(6 I / not go)** .... walking without waterproofs, a basic first aid kit and extra food. That way, if **(7 I / have)** .... an accident, **(8 I / be)** .... OK while I waited for a rescue.

If you have time

Find the nine letter word. How many words can you make with the letters?

E	D	R	V	A	N	U	T	E

Working with words: verb + noun

1 Look at the examples. Think of two more nouns we use after *ride* and *drive*.

I ride a bike to school.
My dad drives a lorry at work.

⇒⇒ **See Working with words, Page 123** ⟩

Speaking

2 Look at the words in the box. How many other forms of transport do you know?

a canoe	a catamaran	a ferry	a hovercraft
a jeep	a lorry	a mountain bike	a ship
a taxi	a tram	the underground	

3 Work in pairs. How many forms of transport would you use to get from your town to London? Use some of these verbs and some nouns from Exercise 2. Repeat for three more destinations.

climb	cycle	drive	fly	hike	ride	sail
take	trek	walk				

A: *I would take a bus to the airport.*
B: *OK, but first I would ride my bike to the bus station.*

Listening

CHECK IT!

4 🔘 **8.3** Listen to three conversations. Where are the people? Write the numbers (1–3) next to three places. There is one extra place.

at an airport on a ferry in a taxi
at an underground railway station

5 🔘 **8.3** Listen again and complete the information.

1 Train line: _____ Ticket price: _____
2 Flight time: _____ Gate number: _____
3 Arrival time: _____ Price of ticket: _____

6 Match these notices with two of the places in Exercise 4.

1 Don't throw litter into the water.

2 Please do not talk to the driver during the journey.

Reading and listening

STUDY SKILLS

7 Read the text quickly and choose the best title.

a The London Underground
b How to travel without a map
c A history of maps

How would we travel without maps? It would be a bit adventurous to set off from Oxford Circus to go to London Bridge if there wasn't a map of the London Underground at each station. In fact, a lot of the early map-makers were adventurers and explorers, especially in the 15th and 16th centuries.

So what did people do before there were maps? Well, it was quite easy to use natural features like mountains and valleys if you were travelling on foot or riding a horse. People sailed small boats down rivers and followed coastlines. And it was much more logical to use time, not distance, to measure journeys: the next village is a three-hour ride, for example. In some cultures, people used spoken instructions to pass on information, like the 'song lines' of the Aboriginal Australians, and special poetry in India.

In fact, in the earliest maps, people didn't draw landmarks. They drew the arrangement of the stars. It was very easy to see the night sky and use it for navigation. The sky was a lot clearer before the light pollution from cities that we have today. When towns and cities were built, people drew road maps which gave correct distances and directions.

STUDY SKILLS

8 ⊙ **8.4 Read and listen to the text. Complete the sentences.**

1 It wasn't _____ to use natural features for navigation.

2 These days, we _____ see as many stars in the sky because of light pollution.

3 The train companies didn't _____ Beck's new map at first.

The London Underground was opened in 1863 and it also used a road map style. But a man called Henry Beck realised that travelling by train isn't the same as driving your car across London. Passengers only needed to know which stations to change at. His new design for the Underground map wasn't very popular with the train companies at first. But the passengers loved it and in 1933, 700,000 copies were printed.

These days, of course, you can run, trek or ride a bike across a desert and know your exact position, using GPS. It's really difficult to get lost!

Grammar: quantifiers + adjectives

9 Look at the text and complete these sentences.

1 It would be _____ adventurous to set off from Oxford Circus.

2 In fact, _____ the early map-makers were adventurers and explorers.

3 It was _____ easy to use natural features.

4 It was _____ more logical to use time.

5 His new design wasn't _____ popular at first.

6 It's _____ difficult to get lost!

10 Complete the table with *a lot, much, really, quite* and *very*.

_____ , _____ ,	+ adjective
_____ , a bit	
_____ , _____ ,	+ comparative
a bit	adjective

 See Grammar GPS, Page 131

11 Choose the correct option.

1 Trekking in the Himalayas would be *very / a lot* dangerous.

2 A beach holiday would be *quite / much* boring.

3 A cruise around the Mediterranean would be *a lot / really* interesting.

4 A safari would be *much / very* better than a trip to a theme park.

5 A train journey would be *a bit / very* more exciting than a helicopter trip.

Speaking

12 Work in groups of four. Discuss the sentences in Exercise 11. Do you agree with the opinions? Give your own opinions.

STUDY SKILLS

Reading a text

1 Before you read a text, you should know why you're reading it. Which of these things do you want to do?

- answer a question
- look for detailed information
- get the general idea/topic
- find out the writer's purpose
- learn new vocabulary
- read for pleasure

2 Choose a helpful strategy for your purpose. Look through the study skills boxes in previous units to help you.

Reading and listening

1 **8.5** Read and listen to the dialogue. What is the problem?

a Jack can't find Lee.

b Reem has lost the room key.

c They don't know where their teacher is.

2 Read the dialogue again. Where have Jack, Reem and Lauren looked for Mrs Taylor? Why are they looking for her?

3 <u>Underline</u> ways of saying these things in the dialogue:

offering help

requesting information

giving advice

making suggestions

giving instructions

Receptionist:	Hello. What can I do for you?
Jack:	Could you give us the room number of Mrs Taylor, please?
Receptionist:	Is she a guest here at the hotel?
Lauren:	Yes, she's our teacher.
Receptionist:	And the arrival date?
Jack:	We arrived yesterday.
Receptionist:	Here we are … room 602. Would you like me to call the room?
Reem:	Yes, please. That would be great.
Receptionist:	There's no answer. She's not in her room, I'm sorry.
Lauren:	Oh dear. We need to speak to her.
Receptionist:	If I were you, I'd look in the restaurant. She's probably having breakfast.

Reem:	We've already been there. She's not there.
Lauren:	She's not in the gift shop either.
Receptionist:	Why don't you leave a message? I wouldn't worry if I were you.
Jack:	It's all right, thanks. We'll manage.
Receptionist:	Oh, have you tried the gym?
Reem:	No … can you tell us where it is?
Receptionist:	Go through those doors and down the stairs. Don't turn left or you'll be in the kitchens!
Lauren:	Thanks. Jack, you should go back to your room and look after Lee. Make sure he's OK. We'll look in the gym.

4 ◯ **8.6** Listen and repeat the *Useful expressions*. Focus on your intonation.

Useful expressions

Could you **give us the room number of Mrs Taylor, please?**
Don't **turn left** or you'll **be in the kitchens!**
If I were you, I'd **look in the restaurant.**
What can I do for you?
Why don't you **leave a message?**
Would you like me to **call the room?**
You should **go back to your room.**

CHECK IT!

5 Match the questions (1–4) with the answers (a–e). There is one extra answer.

1 Could you tell me where the shop is, please?
2 Would you like me to carry your bags?
3 What's the best way of getting to the zoo?
4 It's very hot today. Perhaps a boat trip isn't a good idea.

a If I were you, I'd take the underground.
b You should set off as soon as possible.
c Yes, of course. It's next to the restaurant.
d Yes, please. They're quite heavy.
e Why don't you go to the Natural History Museum instead?

Writing: holiday tips

1 Read Ben's tips for Lee's trip to the USA. Tick the things he talks about.

money   packing   passports   sightseeing
tickets   vaccinations

2 Underline *in case*, *or* and *unless* in the email. Which tenses follow them?

 **See Grammar GPS, Page 131**

3 Complete the sentences with *in case*, *or* or *unless*.

1 You'll need a return ticket .... you won't be allowed into the country.
2 You won't be allowed in .... you have a return ticket.
3 Take some travel tablets .... you get travel sick.

4 Write tips for travellers to your country or to a country you know. Use the ideas in Exercise 1 and the words in Exercise 2.

CHECK IT!

6 ◯ **8.7** Listen to a conversation (1) and an answerphone message (2), and complete the information.

	1	2
Guest's name:	....	Mrs Watson
Type of room:	single	?
Length of stay:	....	....
Arrival date:	....	....

Speaking

7 Work in pairs. You are the receptionist and a guest at a hotel in London. Write dialogues for these situations. Take turns. Then take a role each and practise your dialogues.

You've lost your passport.
There's a spider in your bath.
You need advice about sightseeing.
You want to change some money.

Pronunciation: difficult words

8 How do you pronounce these words? Compare with your partner.

answer   biscuit   business   calm   castle
comfortable   foreign   mountain   restaurant
through   woman   women

9 ◯ **8.8** Listen and repeat the words in Exercise 8.

To: <Lee>
From: <Ben>
Subject: Your visit

Hi Lee,

I'm really pleased that you're coming to the States this summer. It'll be great! There's lots to do, so you should start to get organised. The first thing is to check that your passport is valid or you won't be able to get into the country. That would be terrible! I don't think you'll need a visa unless you stay for more than three months. (It would be great if you could, but I guess two weeks is good too.) What else? It's a good idea to change some money before you come. And bring some hiking gear in case we decide to go camping.

And don't forget your camera or you won't have any sightseeing photos to show your mum when you get back!

Anyway, I'll write more later. Here's my cellphone number (7955846745) in case you want to text me.

See you soon,

Ben

The Caribbean: a tourist paradise

Reading

1 Work in pairs. Look at the photos. Would you like to go to these places and do these things? Why? / Why not?

Culture

Caribbean Islands

The Caribbean is many people's idea of paradise – beautiful beaches, fantastic wildlife and great weather. But what's it like to live there?

The original name of **Jamaica** meant 'land of wood and water', but perhaps it should be 'land of music and sport'. Jamaica is famous for its music and is the home of athletes Usain Bolt and Asafa Powell. But unfortunately not everybody can be world-famous. Most people work in jobs that are related to the tourist industry or farming. So although Jamaica is a beautiful place, people who want to do something different with their lives often emigrate to the USA or the UK.

It's a good idea to learn to swim if you live in the **Bahamas**. The sea around the islands is crystal clear and quite shallow – which is perfect for sharks. But you shouldn't be afraid of sharks. This is one of the few places in the world where you can swim with (and feed!) sharks. The fishing and diving resorts attract a lot of tourists, and the islands' economy depends on this kind of tourism. Local businesses have to work hard to protect this natural environment.

A new kind of tourism called 'ecotourism' is increasing in some parts of the Caribbean. It focuses on giving employment to local young people so that they don't need to emigrate. In the **Virgin Islands**, for example, the Sustainable Farm Institute is the alternative to more traditional tourist resorts. Local people learn how to start their own farms – which will give their families work in the future – and tourists come to stay on the farm and experience more than just a beach holiday.

2 🔘 **8.9 Read about some of the Caribbean islands. Where would you go to do these things?**

1 feed a shark

2 have an 'eco-holiday'

3 stay on a working farm

4 see the homes of famous sportsmen

3 **Read the text again and answer the questions.**

1 Why do people from Jamaica go to the USA or the UK?

2 What kinds of activities do tourists go to the Bahamas for?

3 Why is ecotourism good for the Virgin Islands? (two reasons)

4 **Find words in the text which match the definitions.**

1 leave your country to live in a different one

2 not very deep

3 the money of a country from business, industry and tourism

4 jobs and work

Listening

5 🔘 **8.10 Listen to Paul talking about his holiday in the Caribbean. Tick the activities he mentions.**

cooking   diving   fishing
lying on the beach   sightseeing
sunbathing   swimming   working

6 🔘 **8.10 Listen again and answer the questions.**

1 Where did Paul stay?

a at a friend's house

b in a hotel

c on a farm

2 What was different about his holiday?

a He worked.

b It was free.

c He never went to the beach.

3 Where did he go at the end of his holiday?

a on a fishing trip

b to a tropical forest

c to the capital city

Geography and English

Geotourism

1 **What do you think 'geotourism' is?**

a visits to volcanoes and other geological sites of interest

b tourism which protects natural places such as forests

c tourism which doesn't harm places where tourists go

2 **Read about geotourism and check your answer to Exercise 1.**

What is geotourism?

Geotourism is a kind of tourism that protects and respects the places where tourists go. Ecotourism focuses on the natural environment. Geotourism also protects historic sites and local culture. It is a kind of tourist activity that helps local people and their economy but does not destroy it.

What is the Geotourism Challenge?

The National Geographic Society organises a competition every year. It looks at tourist resorts around the world and chooses the ones which are most successful in geotourism. Recently the Sustainable Farm Institute in the Virgin Islands was a finalist in the competition.

What are geotourism projects?

These are places where geotourism is already successful – where local governments, tourist businesses and local people work together to develop their tourist industry. There are also 'planned projects', where people have agreed to the ideas, but they are still developing their geotourism activities.

- Geotourism projects

- Planned geotourism projects

- Geotourism challenge finalists

3 **Look at the map and the key. What happens at the places marked by the coloured dots?**

Project ▶▶

Work in groups. Make a list of the main tourist areas in your region or your country. Find or draw a map and mark the different kinds of tourism on the map.

Reading

1 Read the airport notices. <u>Underline</u> the words which tell you the notice is at an airport.

1 **Passport control and gates 1–30 this way**

2 **Flight arrivals and departures information** ↑

2 Read these notices and <u>underline</u> the key words.

a **Holiday offers. Click here to find out prices and destinations.**

b Follow the marked paths. Do not disturb young animals. ↗

c Downstairs to gym, conference rooms and sauna.

d No photographs. No food. Do not touch the exhibits.

3 Write places where you can see the notices in Exercise 2.

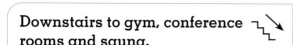

CHECK IT!

4 Match the signs (a–d) in Exercise 2 with the places (1–5). There is one extra place.

  1 in a museum
  2 on a webpage
  3 in a shop
  4 in a hotel
  5 in a national park

Listening

1 Write words and expressions you might hear in conversations in these places.

  1 at a hotel reception desk
  2 at a theatre booking office
  3 at a railway station
  4 in a restaurant

2 Where would you hear people say these things?

  a I'd like the soup, please.
  b I'm sorry, there aren't any tickets left.
  c How many nights are you staying?
  d Do you want a single or a return ticket?

3 Think of questions for *a* and *b*, and responses for *c* and *d* in Exercise 2.

4 ◉ *8.11* Listen to the conversations and match them with three of the places in Exercise 1.

5 ◉ *8.12* Listen to the announcement. Which group of words do you hear?

  a flight   passengers   gate
  b passenger   train   late
  c Manchester   delay   buses

6 Where is the announcement in Exercise 5?

  a at an airport
  b at a railway station
  c at a bus station

CHECK IT!

7 ◉ *8.13* Listen to the answerphone message. Where is it from? Choose the correct option (a–c).

  a hotel
  b a travel agency
  c a clothes shop

Spelling: words with the /s/ sound

1 Complete the words with the letter combinations in the box.

ce	ci	cy	sc	se	ss

1 appearan_____

2 emergen_____

3 fa_____inating

4 ni_____

5 po_____ible

6 _____rtain

7 exerci_____

8 increa_____

9 parti_____pant

10 sen_____

Spelling: making adverbs from adjectives

2 Write the adverb.

1 bored _____

2 extreme _____

3 heavy _____

4 independent _____

5 dramatic _____

6 enormous _____

7 full _____

8 incredible _____

9 possible _____

10 unfortunate _____

Punctuation: joining sentences with commas

3 Add commas (,) to these sentences if necessary.

1 I'd go on a cruise round the Mediterranean if I could afford it.

2 Most large cities such as London and Paris have an underground rail system.

3 There are some great things to see in Egypt like the Great Pyramid or Luxor.

4 Although it was quicker to go by plane we decided to travel by train.

5 If I were you I'd take a jacket in case it rains.

4 Join the sentences with a linking word from the box. Add a comma if necessary.

and	but	even though	or	so

1 I've packed clothes for wet weather _____ for hot and sunny weather.

2 We've arrived at the hotel _____ we haven't checked in yet.

3 We got to the airport late _____ we missed the plane.

4. Shall we go take the Underground _____ shall we walk?

5 We had a great holiday _____ it rained every day!

Writing an email: personal news

5 Imagine your family recently won a holiday to somewhere exciting. Write notes about the following in your notebook.

- What did you do to win the holiday?
- Where are you going?
- What is it like there?
- How are you getting there?
- Where are you going to stay?
- What are you going to do while you are there?

6 Write an email to a friend, telling them the news about the holiday.

Use the layout below to organise your ideas into three short paragraphs.

Look at the *Useful expressions* in the *Writing bank* below. Also, look at the *Useful expressions* for writing personal emails in Unit 1.

Paragraph 1: Ask your friend something about him/herself – maybe they have been on holiday or just sat some exams.

Paragraph 2: Tell them your exciting news about winning the holiday. Use your notes in Exercise 7.

Paragraph 3: Invite your friend to join your family on the holiday.

Paragraph 4: Say goodbye and tell your friend to write soon.

7 Work in pairs. Read your partner's letter and tick the checklist.

Has your partner:
- written an interesting letter?
- organised the letter into paragraphs?
- joined sentences using the correct punctuation?
- correctly used *the* for referring back?

8 If your partner invited you to go with them on the holiday, would you accept? Why/ Why not?

Spelling: words with the /s/ sound

Most words which are pronounced with an unvoiced /s/ are spelled with the single letter *c* or double *s* (*ss*).

Words with single letter *c* (soft *c*)
Words ending in *ce* are pronounced /s/

advice	chance	experience	office	science

Words with *c* + *e*, i or *y*

circle	cycle	decide	excellent	face	price
receive	space	success			

Words ending with a double *s* (*ss*)

Words ending with a vowel + *ss* are pronounced /s/.

across	address	class	discuss	fitness
glass	helpless	lesson	mess	pass

Words with double *ss* between two vowels

messy	classical	message

Note the exceptions: dessert, possess, scissors
    (the *ss* is pronounced /z/)

Words spelled with a single *s* + *e* to make the /s/ sound

course	decrease	else	false	horse	house
mouse	purchase	tense	universe	worse	

Sometimes the /s/ sound is spelled with *s* + silent *c* or *t*

fascinating	muscle	scene	science	castle	listen	whistle

Note the exception: rescue (The *c* is not silent.)

ise* or *ize*?

In British English the following verbs always end in *ise*:

advise	exercise	promise	revise	surprise.

Both spellings are acceptable with:

finalise/ize	organise/ize	realise/ize.

Spelling: adjectives and adverbs endings

To make an adverb, add the correct ending to the adjective.

Add *ly*

You add *ly* to most adjectives, including words ending in *l*:

careful	carefully	extreme	extremely
nervous	nervously	surprising	surprisingly

Note the exception: after double *l* (*ll*), add *y*: full fully

After *y*

Change the *y* to *i* and add *ly*.

easy	easily	happy	happily
lucky	luckily		

After *able/ible*

Remove the *e* and add *ay*.

reasonable	reasonably	terrible	terribly

After *ic*

Add *ally*.

economic	economically	genetic	genetically

Punctuation: joining sentences

We use commas (,) to join sentences in the following ways:

sentence + , + linking word + sentence

When we join two sentences with a linking word, we usually put a comma after the first sentence when each of the sentences includes a subject.
I went to Italy last summer, and I'm going there again.

I got up late, but I still got to school on time!

I might go to Greece this year, or I might go to Spain

I felt ill on the boat, even though the sea was calm.

I felt seasick, so I took a travel tablet.

Note: *so* in the last sentence means *as a result*. When *so* means *in order to*, you do not use a comma.

Close the window so the rain doesn't come in.

sentence + linking word + sentence

If the second sentence is not a complete sentence because the subject is not repeated, a comma is not needed before *and* or *but*. Compare these sentences:
I got up late but still got to school on time!
I got up late, but I still got to school on time!
If you are in doubt, add a comma.

With conditional sentences and *although*

 *See Grammar GPS, Pages 127 and 131*

Before giving examples

We use a comma after phrases which introduce the examples: *for example, such as, for instance, that is.* You put a comma between the example items, but not before *or* and *and*, which separate the last two items. We usually put a comma before *but not*, as this shows a contrast.
There are many old cities such as Rome, Athens or Cairo.

You will see lots of animals there, including lions and bears.

You can do lots of sports on the lake, like canoeing, sailing, but not windsurfing.

Listing

The same rules apply as for giving examples above.
We can't decide whether to go to camping, rent an apartment or stay in a hotel.

Useful expressions: talking about news

Asking about news
How's school? How was the school trip?
How did your exams/driving test go?
Have you taken your driving test yet?

Giving news
Guess what? I've just got back from fantastic weekend!
I've got some great news!
By the way, I've got a spare ticket.
Actually, there's something (else) I want to tell you.

Grammar consolidation
Easily confused words → See Grammar GPS, Page 132

Possessive adjectives and possessive pronouns

This is her bike. = This bike is hers.

1 Read the first sentence. Complete the second sentence with a possessive pronoun.

1 The blue bike is Jack's. It's _____ .
2 This is our dog. She's _____ .
3 'Is this your book?' 'Yes, it's _____ .'
4 'Is that their house?' 'Yes, it's _____ .'
5 Is this your jacket? Or is the green one _____ ?
6 The red hat is Emma's. It's _____ .

There + be and It + be

We use *there* to introduce something. We use *it* when we refer to the thing for a second time. We also use *it + be* with adjectives and prepositions.

2 Choose the correct option.

(1) *There / It* was very hot yesterday. (2) *There / It* was a fire in the forest. (3) *There / It* was very dangerous. (4) *There / It* was very difficult to put out the fire. (5) *There / It* was a special report about it on TV.

3 Complete the dialogue with *there* or *it*.

Yusuf:	Hey, (1) _____'s a writing competition at school.
Ayman:	I know! (2) _____'s on the school website.
Yusuf:	Is (3) _____ a good prize?
Ayman:	Yes, (4) _____'s a trip to an outdoor centre called *Wild Skills*.
Yusuf:	Oh, yes. (5) _____'s a great climbing wall there. I read about it.
Ayman:	So, let's have a go!

Like, be like, look like, to like

We use *like* in different ways. My brother (**a**) looks like me, but he (**b**) isn't like me. He (**c**) likes playing tennis and I like playing team games, (**d**) like football.

4 Complete the table with *a, b, c* and *d* to match the examples of *like* in the sentences above.

to like = a verb	
like = for example	
to look like = physical appearance	
be like = to be similar	

5 Complete the sentences.

1 _____ you _____ science fiction?
2 Who _____ you _____ in your family?
3 _____ your sister _____ you? Or are you very different?
4 Is that Wayne Rooney? It _____ him.
5 Food _____ chips and chocolate is fattening.

6 Match the questions (1–4) with the answers (a–d).

1 What does a tarantula look like?
2 What are tarantulas like?
3 Do you like tarantulas?
4 Would you like a tarantula?

a It's hairy, and it has eight legs.
b No, thanks.
c They're quite frightening, but they aren't always dangerous.
d Yes, I think they're interesting.

7 Write questions for these answers. Use *a snake* or *snakes* in each question.

1 _____ ?
No, I don't think they would be good pets.
2 _____ ?
They are long and thin.
3 _____ ?
No, I don't. I think they're frightening.
4 _____ ?
I think some of them can be aggressive.

Vocabulary

1 Write the words.

1 an area with lots of shops   s....................
                                    c....................

2 thinking of others   c....................

3 rubbish that people drop   l....................

4 a person who offers to help or work for no pay   v....................

5 a place for professional football, etc.   s....................
                                    s....................

1 mark per item: …/5 marks

2 Write the types of holiday.

1 On a _____ , you see wild animals.

2 On a _____ , you live on a ship.

3 There's sea and sand on _____ holidays.

4 On a _____ holiday, you visit places of interest.

5 On _____ holidays, you walk a lot.

1 mark per item: …/5 marks

3 Write the things.

1 ....
2 ....
3 ....
4 ....
5 ....

1 mark per item: …/5 marks

4 Write the transport.

1 ....
2 ....
3 ....
4 ....
5 ....

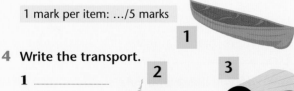

1 mark per item: …/5 marks

5 Complete the sentences with one word.

1 I lost my watch, so I _____ my friend's.

2 Firefighters _____ lives every day.

3 English people _____ usually polite.

4 He speaks French very _____ . He's fluent.

5 I can't _____ a bike.

1 mark per item: …/5 marks

Grammar

6 Report a teacher's words with the verbs.

1 'Sit down, everyone.' (order)

2 'Don't make a noise.' (tell / the class)

3 'Please listen, Jack.' (ask)

4 'Don't be late for the test!' (warn / the class)

5 'Would you like to come to a meeting?' (invite / the parents)

1 mark per item: …/5 marks

7 Are the questions correct (✔) or incorrect (✘)?

1 Can you tell us where is the conference?

2 Do you know is there a park near here?

3 Could you tell me how much the tickets are?

4 Can you tell me if pets are allowed here?

5 Do you know what time the shops close?

1 mark per item: …/5 marks

8 Write sentences with the second conditional.

1 If I _____ a snake, I'd run away. (see)

2 I _____ to South Africa if I had enough money. (go)

3 If I was an explorer, I _____ in this country. (not / live)

4 If I _____ to Jordan, I'd visit Petra. (go)

5 What _____ if you were lost in the Arctic? (you / do)

1 mark per item: …/5 marks

9 Choose the correct option.

1 It's *a bit / much* boring to watch TV all day.

2 A cruise is *quite / much* more expensive than a camping holiday.

3 Climbing Mount Etna is *a lot / quite* hard.

4 Cars are *much / very* faster than bikes.

5 A trip to China would be *a lot / really* exciting.

1 mark per item: …/5 marks

10 Complete the sentences.

1 This camera is John's. It's _____ .

2 This is our house. It's _____ .

3 _____ was a storm here yesterday.

4 That woman _____ like my mum! They've got the same eyes!

5 Ben _____ like his brother. They're both competitive.

1 mark per item: …/5 marks

Communicate!

11 Complete the dialogue with the expressions.

> Could you give him a message?
> You're welcome.
> I'll tell him.
> Can you ask him to …
> With pleasure.

John: Is Ben there please?

Ben's mum: No, he's not here at the moment.

John: (1) ....

Ben's mum: (2) ....

John: (3) ....
call John, please?

Ben's mum: Yes, of course. Has he got your phone number?

John: Yes, he has. But if it's really late, he can send me a text.

Ben's mum: OK, (4) ....

John: Thanks very much.

Ben's mum: (5) ....

2 marks per item: …/10 marks

12 Match the sentences (1–5) with the functions (a–e).

1 Why don't you go by bus?

2 Could you tell me the flight number?

3 If I were you, I'd take a train.

4 Go to Gate 45, in the North terminal.

5 Can I help you with your suitcase?

a giving advice

b making a suggestion

c offering help

d requesting information

e giving instructions

2 marks per item: …/10 marks

13 Are the underlined sounds in each pair the same (S) or different (D)?

1 wo<u>m</u>an   wo<u>m</u>en   ....

2 moun<u>tain</u>   lis<u>ten</u>   ....

3 comfor<u>table</u>   <u>table</u>   ....

4 b<u>u</u>siness   b<u>u</u>s   ....

5 c<u>a</u>lm   <u>a</u>rm   ....

2 marks per item: …/10 marks

14 Complete the sentences with *or, in case* or *unless.*

1 I'm packing some waterproofs .... it rains.

2 Hurry up .... we'll miss the bus.

3 We won't phone you .... we have a problem.

4 Take some insect repellent .... there are mosquitoes.

5 You can't get on the plane .... you have a ticket.

2 marks per item: …/10 marks

15 Complete the email with these words.

> a lot   actually   at   by the way   if I were you
> guess what   luckily   really   to   unfortunately

Dear Lisa,
I'm (**1**) .... pleased that you and your mum are coming to visit us! (**2**) ...., I'd take the bus. It's (**3**) .... cheaper than the train. (**4**) ...., it's quicker too. (**5**) ...., there's only one bus a day. I'll come and meet you (**6**) .... the bus station. (**7**) ....? I've got a new coat and hat! You might not recognise me! (**8**) ...., I hope you like cats – we've got four now. They sometimes fight, but (**9**) ...., they spend a lot of time outside! Don't forget (**10**) .... send me the dates of your visit!
Love,
Emma

1 mark per item: …/10 marks

Total: …/100

I can...

Tick (✔) what you can do.

	★★★★★	★★★	★
I can give and take messages.			
I can offer help.			
I can request information.			
I can give advice.			
I can make suggestions.			
I can give instructions.			

positive adjective ▶ negative adjective

We add *un-* or *im-* to some adjectives to give the opposite meaning.

friendly   unfriendly

1 Add *un-* or *im-* to *happy* and *possible* and write them in the correct place in the table.

un-		im-
uncomfortable	unkind	immature
unfit	unlucky	impatient
unfriendly	unnecessary	impolite
	unsuccessful	
unhealthy	untidy	
unimportant		

2 Choose the correct option.

1 I'm *lucky / unlucky*. I always win.

2 Wait a moment! Don't be *patient / impatient*.

3 Are you OK? You don't seem *happy / unhappy*.

4 It's *polite / impolite* to say 'thank you'.

5 Mrs Jones is very *kind / unkind* and helpful.

3 Complete the sentences with adjectives from the table in Exercise 1.

1 This sofa is very _____ .

2 I can't do this maths homework. It's _____ !

3 I love chocolate and other _____ food.

4 My brother is 16, but he's very _____ .

5 I never do sports. I'm _____ .

4 Complete the sentences with adjectives from the table in Exercise 1.

1 You don't have to do this. It's _____ .

2 Your bedroom is a mess. It's _____ .

3 Your neighbours never speak to you. They're _____ .

4 It doesn't matter. It's _____ .

5 You're not doing well. You're _____ .

Working on your own

5 What are the negative forms of these adjectives? We add *un-*, *in-* or *ir-* to some of them. Check in a dictionary.

available	correct	intelligent	natural
regular	responsible		

do and *make*

We use *do* and *make* with different nouns.

We're doing a project.   I'm making a cake.

1 Write the words in the correct place in the table.

maths	a model	a sandwich	the shopping

do	make
an exam	my bed
an experiment	breakfast
exercise	a cake
history	friends
homework	a mess
gymnastics	a mistake
a project	a noise
	a phone call
sports	a pizza
a test	
the washing up	a sculpture

2 Look at the table in Exercise 1 and choose the correct option.

1 We often use *do / make* with schoolwork.

2 We often use *do / make* with food and meals.

3 Complete the sentences with *do* or *make*.

1 Do you _____ gymnastics at school?

2 Can you _____ a pizza?

3 Do you have to _____ an exam today?

4 When do you _____ your homework?

5 What subjects do you _____ at school?

4 Write sentences about your family.

▶ ___*My dad does*___ the washing up.

1 _____ my bed.

2 _____ breakfast.

3 _____ cakes.

4 _____ the shopping.

Working on your own

5 In your notebook, write your own sentence with *do* or *make* and each of these words.

exercises	a mistake	a phone call	a project

nouns ▶ adjectives

We can add endings to nouns to make adjectives.

artist – artistic
fame – famous
success – successful
talent – talented
tradition – traditional

1 Make adjectives from these nouns and write them in the correct place in the table.

danger   interest   music   symbol   use

artistic	famous	surprised
volcanic	poisonous	talented
beautiful	industrial	
successful	logical	
	traditional	
	tropical	

Note the spelling changes: beauty – beautiful, fame – famous.

2 Which adjectives from the table in Exercise 1 can you use to describe these people and things?

1 pop singers
2 traditional music
3 mobile phones
4 film stars
5 Formula 1

3 Complete the sentences with adjectives from the table in Exercise 1.

1 My ambition is to be a _____ musician.
2 I was _____ when I won the talent competition.
3 A bite from a _____ snake can kill you.
4 Hurricanes are a kind of _____ storm.
5 Burgers are _____ of the USA.

Working on your own

4 Make adjectives from these nouns. Check in a dictionary.

adventure   energy   environment   power   virus

5 Choose five adjectives from the table in Exercise 1. In your notebook, write your own sentence with each adjective.

nouns and verbs ▶ nouns

We can add endings to nouns and verbs to make other nouns.

guitar – guitarist   sing – singing

1 Complete the words in the table.

Nouns		Nouns
art	-ist	an art_____
a piano		a pianist
a violin		a violinist
drums	-er	a drummer

Verbs		Nouns
communicate	-ion	communication
compete		a competition
connect		a connect_____
educate		educat_____
exhibit		an exhibit_____
protect		protect_____
construct		construct_____
pollute		pollution
paint	-ing	painting
write		writing
compose	-er/-or	a composer
conduct		a conductor
paint		a paint_____
perform		a perform_____
play		a play_____
ski		a skier
write		a write_____
perform	-ance	a performance
appear		an appearance

2 Find twelve nouns in the table for people.

3 Choose the correct option.

1 A pop concert is *a competition / an exhibition / a performance*.
2 Building a house is *protection / construction / pollution*.
3 Pictures in a gallery are *a competition / an exhibition / an appearance*.
4 A musician, singer or actor is *a conductor / a performer / a player*.
5 A telephone conversation is *an appearance / communication / education*.

Working on your own

4 Write the nouns from these words. Use a dictionary.

a guitar   a piano   compose   infect   vaccinate

noun + noun

We can use two nouns together to make another noun. This is called a compound noun.

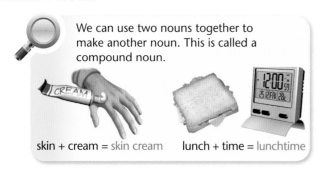

skin + cream = skin cream   lunch + time = lunchtime

1 Match these nouns to make compound nouns. Which compound noun is one word?

art	bed	food	music	rugby
gallery	room	room	team	technology

2 Complete the compound nouns in the table with these words.

bandage	infection	killer	player	story	virus

Two words	One word
cough medicine	earache
ear drops	earpiece
energy drink	headache
flu _____	holidaymaker
honey _____	pain _____
junk food	toothache
news _____	
skin cream	
skin _____	
tennis _____	

3 Look at the table in Exercise 2 and find the names of these things.

Working on your own

4 Choose five compound nouns from Exercises 1 and 2. In your notebook, write your own sentence with each noun.

adjective + preposition

We often use prepositions after adjectives of emotions and feelings.

He's afraid of mice.   She's pleased with her grade.

1 Write the prepositions in the correct place in the table.

about	at	with

afraid of	frightened of
angry with	good _____
annoyed with	happy about / with
bad at	interested in
bored _____	pleased with
confused by	tired of
fed up with	worried _____

2 Some expressions have similar meanings. Which expressions can you also use in these sentences?

1 Are you <u>frightened of</u> vaccinations?
2 Are you <u>happy with</u> your grades?
3 Are you <u>tired of</u> this exercise?
4 Are you <u>angry with</u> anyone at the moment?

3 Read the first sentence. Then complete the second sentence with an appropriate expression from Exercise 1.

1 My dad likes science.
He's _____ .
2 I didn't understand the beginning of the film.
I was _____ .
3 I always get bad grades in maths.
I'm _____ .
4 I think my friend needs some help.
I'm _____ .
5 I usually win tennis matches.
I'm _____ .

Working on your own

4 Do you know what these adjective + preposition combinations mean? Check in a dictionary. In your notebook, write your own sentence with each combination.

ashamed of   excited about   nervous about
proud of   scared of

adjective + noun

There are some adjectives and nouns that we often use together.

a digital camera   a wild animal

1 Write the nouns in the correct place in the table.

activity   friend   phone

a bad habit	a living thing
a bad mood	a natural disaster
a best _____	a mobile _____
a digital camera	a tropical disease
free time	a violent movement
global warming	volcanic activity
a healthy lifestyle	a volcanic eruption
human _____	a wild animal
the industrial age	

2 Answer the questions with words from the table in Exercise 1.

1 What are lions, tigers and giraffes?

2 What are volcanoes, floods and hurricanes?

3 When did people start producing greenhouse gases?

4 How were the Canary Islands formed?

3 Complete the questions with words from the table in Exercise 1.

1 Have you got a _____ lifestyle?

2 Do you tell your _____ friend everything?

3 Do you have a lot of _____ time at the weekend?

4 What are your _____ habits?

5 Have you got a _____ phone?

Working on your own

4 Cover the table in Exercise 1. Complete the adjective + noun combinations. Then check your answers in the table in Exercise 1.

1 a digital _____

2 global _____

3 a living _____

4 a tropical _____

5 In your notebook, write your own sentence with each combination in Exercise 4.

words with two meanings

There are some words in English that have two or more meanings. Sometimes they are the same type of word (eg both nouns) but sometimes they are different (eg a noun and a verb)

She sang in the show.   I'll show you my new horse.

1 Match the word in italics in each sentence with the correct definitions (a or b).

1 I prefer *still* water.

2 The lake is very *still* today.

   a not moving   **b** not fizzy

3 The film is *over*.

4 There are *over* sixty lions in the zoo.

   a finished   **b** more than

5 I'm not very *fit*.

6 It doesn't *fit*. It's too small.

   a in good physical shape   **b** be the right size

2 Choose the best picture (a or b) for each sentence.

1 He gave his wife a ring from the office.

2 She wrote lots of notes to help her study for her exams.

3 They sat on the bank and ate their picnic.

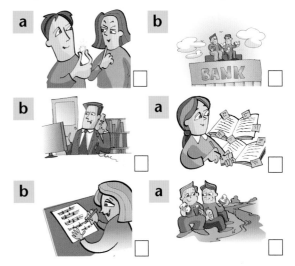

Working on your own

3 Do you know two different meanings for these words? Check in a dictionary and write a sentence for each of the meanings.

around   diet   flat   light   notice

compound adjectives

Compound adjectives are made of two words. The words are connected by a hyphen (-).

He seems
bad-tempered.

He's always
well-dressed.

1 Complete the adjectives in the table with these words.

dressed	eyed	looking	minded

bad-tempered	self-centred
blue-_____	self-confident
brown-haired	solar-powered
easy-going	three-storey
good-_____	well-_____
old-fashioned	world-famous
open-_____	

2 Which one word can you use to make adjectives with these words?

black	blond	brown	curly	dark	long
red	short	straight			

3 Complete the sentences with adjectives from the table in Exercise 1.

1 Your dad accepts new ideas.
He's _____ .

2 Your mum prefers things / ideas from the past. She's _____ .

3 Your sister thinks about herself a lot. She's
_____ .

4 Your parents let you do what you want.
They're _____ .

5 Your brother isn't afraid of new situations.
He's _____ .

4 Work in pairs. Name a person or thing for each adjective. You must agree.

old-fashioned	self-confident	solar-powered
three-storey	world-famous	

Working on your own

5 Choose five adjectives from the table in Exercise 1. In your notebook, write your own sentence with each adjective.

phrasal verbs for relationships

Phrasal verbs have two parts: a verb and a preposition. The meaning is usually different from the meaning of the two parts on their own.

I fell and broke my leg.

I fell out with my best friend.

1 Read the sentences and write the prepositions in the correct place in the table.

1 I get on well with my sister.

2 I take after my dad.

3 She made up with her friend.

make _____ (with somebody)	look up to (somebody)
fall out (with somebody)	make up (with somebody)
get _____ (with somebody)	take _____ (somebody)
look after (somebody)	

2 Match the phrasal verbs (1–5) with the meanings (a–e).

1 take after	**a**	argue with somebody
2 fall out	**b**	respect
3 get on	**c**	be similar to
4 look up to	**d**	have a good relationship
5 make up	**e**	make friends again after an argument

3 Complete the paragraph with phrasal verbs.

Rabi'ah and Sharifa met at school. They
(1) _____ well. They became best friends and **(2)** _____ each other. For example, they helped each other with homework and shared their lunch. They sometimes
(3) _____ with each other, but they always **(4)** _____ afterwards.

4 Complete the sentences with the prepositions.

1 I look _____ my big brother – he's great.

2 My mum looked _____ me when I was ill.

3 I take _____ my dad – we're both tall.

Working on your own

5 Cover the table in Exercise 1. Match these verbs and prepositions. Then check your answers in the table.

fall	get	look	make	take
after	on	out	up	up to

verb + preposition

Some verbs are followed by prepositions.

I'm thinking about my lunch.

I'm talking to my best friend.

1 Write *of, with* and *to* in the correct place in the table.

agree _____	learn about
apologise for	pay for
argue with	talk about
believe in	talk _____
come from	think about
complain about	think of
consist _____	wait for
fight with	work on
know about	worry about
last for	

2 Complete the sentences with prepositions.

1 I don't fight _____ my brother.

2 Have you paid _____ that DVD yet?

3 My sister never agrees _____ me.

4 Who do you argue _____ most?

5 My headset consists _____ a microphone and headphones.

3 Choose the correct preposition.

1 'What do you think *about / of* the *Star Trek* film?' 'It's good.'

2 'What are you thinking *about / of*?' 'My lunch.'

3 'Who are you talking *about / to*?' 'My sister. She's phoning from London.'

4 'What are you talking *about / to*?' 'The *Star Trek* film.'

4 Complete the sentences with different verbs. The preposition is the same in each case.

1 I don't _____ anything about Mars.

2 We _____ about volcanoes today.

3 Don't _____ about me. I'm fine.

Working on your own

5 In your notebook, write your own sentence with each verb + preposition combination.

come from   complain about   work on

phrasal verbs

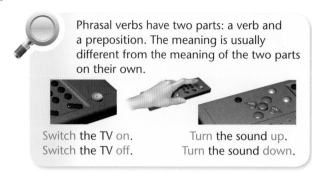

Phrasal verbs have two parts: a verb and a preposition. The meaning is usually different from the meaning of the two parts on their own.

Switch the TV on.
Switch the TV off.

Turn the sound up.
Turn the sound down.

1 Look at the pictures above and write the prepositions in the correct place in the table.

come back	pick up	switch _____
find out	set off	take over
get back	switch off	turn _____
go back		turn up

2 Complete the requests with phrasal verbs from the table in Exercise 1.

1 That's very loud! Could you _____ the volume, please?

2 It's dark. _____ a light.

3 Class is finished. _____ your computers now.

4 I can't hear the TV. Can you _____ the sound?

3 Read the first sentence. Choose the correct option.

1 Robots are taking over the world. They are *in control / exploring*.

2 How did you find out the telephone number? How did you *phone / discover* it?

3 What time did you set off this morning? When did you *drive / leave*?

4 I'll pick up my DVD from your house tonight. I'll *choose / collect* it.

4 Match the sentences (1–3) with the responses (a–c).

1 My parents have gone on holiday.

2 My cousins from Canada are visiting us.

3 I leave for school at 8.30.

a What time do you get back?

b When are they coming back?

c When are they going back?

Working on your own

5 In your notebook, write your own sentence to show the meaning of each phrasal verb.

come back   go back   pick up   set off

easily confused words

There are some words which mean different things but are easy to confuse.

The sun rises in the east.

Raise your arms.

1 Match the sentences (1–5) with the pictures (a–e).

a   b   c   d   e

1 I feel sick.
2 Hold my hand.
3 He's saved that boy's life.
4 Can you tell me the time, please?
5 I'm going to lie down.

2 Complete the sentences with these words.

ill   keep   make   remind   travel

1 _____ me to rent a DVD.
2 Can you _____ a secret?
3 I'm going to _____ a cake.
4 They're _____ . They've got flu.
5 Does she _____ a lot in her job?

3 Choose the correct option.

1 Come to my party! *Bring / Take* a friend!
2 Let's go for a walk. Let's *bring / take* the dogs.
3 Is the skate park *safe / save* for children?
4 My house was *robbed / stolen* during the night.
5 Can you *lend / borrow* me a pencil?

Working on your own

4 Use your dictionary. Write translations of these words.

borrow / lend	journey / travel / trip
bring / take	lay / lie
come back / go back	raise / rise
do / make	recall / remind
hold / keep	safe / save
ill / sick	say / tell

5 In your notebook, write your own sentence with each word in Exercise 4.

irregular nouns

The plural form of most nouns ends in -s. Some nouns are irregular.

people   children

1 Some plural nouns have irregular spelling. Choose the correct option.

1 How *much / many* people *live / lives* in your town?
2 *Is / Are* there a lot of children in your street?
3 There *is / are* three women and two men on the team.

2 Some nouns end in -s, but they are singular. Choose the correct option.

1 I think economics *seem / seems* interesting.
2 The news *was / were* surprising.
3 Maths *is / are* our first lesson on Monday.
4 *Is / Are* gymnastics your favourite sport?
5 Physics *isn't / aren't* easy for me.

3 Some nouns don't end in -s, but their meanings can be plural. Complete the sentences with these words.

oryx   committee   family   team   police

1 Are the _____ investigating the crime?
2 There aren't any wild _____ in Europe.
3 Are your _____ coming to see you?
4 The England _____ aren't ready.
5 The _____ are discussing the problem.

Working on your own

4 Write the plural form of these nouns.

bus   country   dish   chief   watch

5 In your notebook, write your own sentence with each plural noun in Exercise 4.

adjective ▶ adverb

 We can add -ly to some adjectives to make adverbs. (Note that not all words which end in -ly are adverbs.) There are some irregular adverbs which don't end in -ly.

1 Make adverbs from these adjectives and write them in the correct place in the table.

Adjective	Adverb
bad	badly
calm	calmly
careful	
careless	
dangerous	
easy	easily
fast	fast
good	well
hard	hard

Adjective	Adverb
late	late
loud	
lucky	luckily
patient	
quick	
quiet	
safe	
slow	

2 Complete the second sentence with an adverb from the table in Exercise 1.

1 Don't eat quickly. Eat .... !

2 Don't drive dangerously. Drive .... !

3 Don't talk loudly. Talk .... !

4 Don't work carelessly. Work .... !

5 Don't behave badly. Behave .... !

3 Choose the correct option.

1 We waited *patient / patiently* for the train.

2 We found the hotel *easy / easily*.

3 After the storm, the sea was *calm / calmly*.

4 The trip was *good / well*.

5 I don't speak French very *good / well*.

4 Complete the sentences with these adverbs.

easily   fast   hard   late   luckily

1 The plane's going to arrive ....

2 This train goes .... !

3 I lost my ticket, but .... the travel agent gave me another one.

4 I've worked .... on my project.

5 I passed my exam ....

Working on your own

5 Choose five adverbs from the table in Exercise 1. In your notebook, write your own sentence with each adverb.

verb + noun

 There are some verbs and nouns that we often use together.

My dad drives a van at work.   I ride a bike to school.

1 Write the nouns in the correct place in the table.

a boat   a car   home   a photo   a plane

Verb	Noun
climb	a mountain, a wall
drive	a bus, ..., a lorry, a tractor, a taxi, a van
have	an accident, a health problem, a meal, a shower
fly	a helicopter, ...
go	............................, on holiday, shopping
play	a game, an instrument, a sport
ride	a bike, a camel, a horse
sail	............................, a ship, a yacht
spend	money, time
take	a bus, a decision, medicine, ..., a plane, a risk, a taxi, a train

2 Cover the table in Exercise 1. Match these verbs and nouns. Check your answers in the table.

climb   drive   fly   ride   sail
a camel   a helicopter   a lorry   a mountain   a ship

3 Complete the sentences.

1 Do you often .... tennis?

2 How do you .... your free time?

3 Where did you .... on holiday?

4 Can you .... a horse?

4 Complete the sentences with the correct form of *have* or *take.*

1 I love .... photos.

2 I .... a painkiller when I had earache.

3 We .... an accident because we weren't careful.

4 You shouldn't .... risks in the sea.

5 I'm hungry. Let's .... lunch.

Working on your own

5 Choose five nouns from the table in Exercise 1. In your notebook, write your own sentence with each noun.

Grammar GPS

UNIT 1

THE PRESENT SIMPLE

Remember that there are two forms for the **present simple**, one for the third person singular, and another for all the others:

I / You / We / They like going for a walk.
He / She / It likes going for a walk.
I / You / We / They don't like going for a walk.
He / She / It doesn't like going for a walk.
Do I / you / he / she / it like going for a walk?
Does he / she / it like going for a walk?

We use the **present simple** to talk about regular habits and things we usually do, for example:

My mother works in a bank.
I don't watch horror films.
Do they eat fish?

a) to talk about regular habits

The **present simple** is frequently used with **adverbs of frequency:**

100% ◄――――――――――――――――――► 0%

always   usually   often   sometimes   occasionally   never

These come after the verb **to be**:

She is never late for school.
Is he always very happy?
They aren't usually so hungry.

but the **adverb of frequency** goes before all other verbs:

They occasionally eat fish for dinner.
We don't usually go to the park on Saturdays.
Do you often read short stories?

We can also use other time expressions with the **present simple**, such as: *every day, every month, once a week, twice a day, three times a year.* These always go at the end of the sentence:

We go to the swimming pool twice a week.
She doesn't ride her bike to work every day.
Do they travel there and back four times a year?

b) to talk about permanent states

We use the **present simple** to talk about our work, the place we live and other things which do not change, for example:

Where does she live? She lives by the sea.
What do you do? I am a doctor.

c) to talk about feelings and thoughts

When we tell someone what we feel or think about a situation, we use the **present simple**, for example:

Do you like it here? No, I don't like this place.
What do you want to do now? I want to go for a swim.
Does he think the film is good? No, he thinks it is too long.

THE PRESENT CONTINUOUS

We make the *present continuous* with the verb **to be** + present participle:

I am sitting in the park at the moment.
You / We / They are sitting in the park at the moment.
He / She / It is sitting in the park at the moment.
I am not / You aren't / He isn't sitting in the park at the moment.
Am I / Are you / Is he sitting in the park at the moment?

We use the **present continuous** to talk about actions which are happening in the period around now – including some time before and after the time of speaking.

I am studying French in the evenings.
They're working in the London office this month.

and things which are happening **at the moment:**

He is in his bedroom at the moment. He's doing his homework.

Look at these situations in which we do not use the **present continuous:**

a) to talk about thoughts and feelings

We do not use the verbs for thoughts and feeling (e.g. *like, love, hate,* etc) and stative verbs (e.g. *understand, need, seem, want, know, prefer,* etc.) in the **present continuous**, so you cannot say:

✗ *I am liking this book.*
✗ *I am not understanding what he is saying.*

For these verbs we use the **present simple**:

I like this book.
I don't understand what he is saying.

b) talking about the senses

We do not usually use verbs of sensing (*see, hear, smell*) in the **present continuous**, so you cannot say:

✗ *What are you hearing? I am hearing someone singing.*
✗ *I am not seeing the boat.*

but use *can + present simple* with them:

What can you hear? I can hear someone singing.
I cannot/can't see the boat.

THE PRESENT SIMPLE and THE PRESENT CONTINUOUS

We use the **present simple** to talk about routines and habits (see above). We use the **present continuous** to talk about things that are happening now and around now (see above).

We can use the **present simple** and the **present continuous** tense together when we want to compare a present situation which is different from the usual one, for example:

We usually spend the summer holidays in France, but this year we're spending two weeks here in Italy.
Tom is tidying his room! He never tidies his room normally.

We use the verb *have got* in the *present simple* to talk about three things:

a) possessions

I have (I've) got 250 DVDs at home.
Has he got a mountain bike?
They haven't got any vegetables in their garden.

b) illnesses

We have (We've) got a bad cold.
Has she got a temperature?
They have not (haven't) got measles.

c) family relationships

I have (I've) got two brothers.
Have they got any children?
Salim has not (hasn't) got a sister.

Grammar GPS

UNIT 2
THERE WAS and THERE WERE

Affirmative	Negative	Interrogative
There was a lot of food at the party. There were a lot of people at the concert.	There was not (wasn't) a lot of food at the party. There were not (weren't) a lot of people at the concert.	Was there a lot of food at the party? Were there a lot of people at the concert?

We often use *there was / were* to ask and answer *How much / many… ?* questions:

How many musicians were there in the band? There were five.
How much time was there between the songs? There was about a minute.

Note the pronunciation of *was* in different situations:

There was /wəz/ an interesting new band playing.
Was /wəz/ there anyone you knew at the theatre? Yes, there was. /wəz/

THE PAST SIMPLE and THE PAST CONTINUOUS

a) We use these two tenses together to describe how one action interrupts another in the past. Notice the use of *when* and *while*, and the different ways in which we can say the same thing.

She was playing her violin when a string broke.
While/When she was playing her violin, a string broke.
A string broke while/when she was playing her violin.

b) The same two tenses are used to show the order in which past actions happened. Look at these two sentences:

When the orchestra arrived, I left the concert hall.
(first action (past simple): *arrived*; second action (past simple): *left*)

When the orchestra arrived, I was leaving the concert hall.
(first action (past continuous): *was leaving*; second action (past simple) *left*)

WHEN, WHILE and DURING

Look at these three similar sentences showing how we use *when*, *while* and *during*.

I hurt my finger when/while I was having my piano lesson.
(One action interrupts another, as in the example in the previous section.)

I hurt my finger during my piano lesson.
(These two sentences have exactly the same meaning, but we do not use a second verb in the clause after *during*.)

I hurt my finger when the piano lid fell on it.
(One action happens before another, as in the example in the previous section.)

THE PRESENT PERFECT

We make the **present perfect** tense with the **present simple** of the verb *to have* + the **past participle** of the main verb.

Affirmative: *I / You / We / They have lived here for a long time.*
 He / She / It has lived here for a long time.

Negative: *I / You / We / They have not (haven't) lived here for a long time.*
 He / She / It has not (hasn't) lived here for a long time.

Interrogative: *Have I / you / we / they lived here for a long time?*
 Has he / she / it lived here for a long time?

Remember that the **past participle** of **regular verbs** is the same as the **past simple** form, and is made by adding *ed* (e.g. *worked, played, asked, studied*). However, many of the most common verbs are irregular, and the past participle may or may not be the same as the past simple form. For example:

The same form:

I made – I have made; I put – I have put; I slept – I have slept

A different form:

I ate – I have eaten; I broke – I have broken; I went – I have gone

We use this tense when we are more interested in the fact of doing something than the specific time of doing it. Compare these two sentences.

Present perfect: *I've played in many concerts in the last ten years.*
Past simple: *I played in two concerts last week.*

We use the **present perfect** with *ever* to ask for general information about the past.

Have you ever played an classical music? Yes, I have. / No, I haven't.

When we ask a question about a specific event in the past we use the **past simple**.

Did you play any classical music in your last concert? Yes, I did. / No, I didn't.

These two tenses are often used together in conversation as follows.

John: *Have you ever been to the Sydney Opera House?*
Mary: *Yes, I have.*
John: *When did you go there?*
Mary: *(I went there) In May last year.*

Note: in spoken English we usually use the contracted form of the verb *to have*:

I've been there several times.
She's played the piano for many years.

And in the negative form we often use *never*:

We've never heard him play.
He's never played his guitar to me.

The pronunciation of *have* and *has* varies depending on whether they are stressed or not.

Have /həv/ you ever been there? Yes, I have /hæv/.
Has /həz/ he heard it? Yes, he has /hæz/.

CONSOLIDATION UNITS 1 and 2
AS … AS

We use the construction *as … adjective … as* to compare two things.

Music is as beautiful as poetry.

We can also do this with *not as … adjective … as*.

This band is not (isn't) as good as the first one.

Notice these ways of making comparisons:

Jazz isn't as popular as pop music.
Jazz is less popular than pop music.
Pop music is more popular than jazz.
Jazz is usually quieter than pop music.
Pop music is usually louder than jazz.

We can also use (*not*) *as ... as ...* with *much* + **uncountable noun** and *many* + **plural countable noun**. For example:

He hasn't got as much time as you (have) to practise.
(uncountable noun)
I've got as many CDs as you (have). (countable noun)
Note: the pronunciation of *as* is always /əz/.

AS, THAN and FROM

We can also use *as* by itself, or together with *the same*.

The new CD sounds the same as their last one.
I met the same people at this concert as I did at the last one.
He played the same guitar as my brother.

We use *than* in many comparative constructions with adjectives:

She's better than her sister at music.

We can also use *different from/to* to make comparisons.

She's totally different from/to her sister.

UNIT 3
JUST + THE PRESENT PERFECT

We use this construction to indicate that something happened in the very recent past:

I've just eaten lunch.
Has he just arrived?

YET, ALREADY + THE PRESENT PERFECT

We use *already* in the affirmative **present perfect** to show that something is completed.

I have already done the shopping.

We can also ask questions with *already*. It usually indicates surprise that the action has been completed, often because it was done very quickly. The second version is more emphatic, with a heavy stress on *already*.

Has he already finished his homework?
Has he finished his homework already?

We use *yet* and *not ... yet* to talk about actions in the time up until this moment.

Have you been to the dentist's yet?
The doctor hasn't seen her yet.

Already and *yet* can appear in the same sentence to talk about completed and uncompleted actions. Look at this conversation:

Mother: *Have you taken your medicine yet?*
Paul: *I've already taken my Vitamin C tablet, but I haven't had my cough syrup yet.*

Note the difference between the use of the verbs *go* and *be* when talking about movement and travel.

Alice has been to the doctor's.
(She went earlier and she is now back at home.)

Alice has gone to the doctor's.
(She went some time ago and is still there.)
Alice went to the doctor's.
(This happened some time in the past.)

FOR and SINCE

We use *for* + the **present perfect simple** to talk about an event in relation to a length or period of time.

Hamid has felt ill for the last week.
Susan hasn't been well for several months.

Phrases we use with *for* are followed by a time period, for example: *for ten years, for an hour, for two days, for a long time, for weeks.*

We use *since* + the **present perfect** to talk about an event in relation to a point in time.
I haven't seen a doctor since I was ten years old.
He hasn't felt well since the holidays.

Phrases we use with *since* are followed by time phrases about a specific point in past time, for example: *since Monday, since three o'clock, since my birthday, since I was a baby, since she went to France, since 2009, since January.*

The pronunciation of *for* is unstressed: /fə/.

THE PRESENT PERFECT vs. THE PAST SIMPLE

Note the different time phrases which are used with these two tenses.

Past simple	Present perfect
I saw him ...	I haven't seen her...
five minutes / an hour / two days ago.	today.
	this week / month / year.
last week / month / year.	for hours / weeks / ages.
at 6.00 p.m. yesterday / on Monday / in May / in 2008.	since yesterday / Sunday / June / 2008.

Look at these sentences to see the difference in use of the **present perfect** and **past simple**.

I'm worried because my grandma is in hospital. She's had an accident.
My grandma's feeling fine now. I'm so happy she's recovered.

(Both sentences comment on a recent event using the **present perfect**. The focus is on the event and its results (an accident – in hospital and now recovered). We do not say when the event happened.

My grandma had an accident last month. I was really worried when she was in hospital. Luckily she recovered very quickly.
(Both sentences narrate a completed past event, using the **past simple**. We normally say when the event/s happened.)

SO and NEITHER

We use these phrases to agree with what someone says positively or negatively. They are formed with the same verb as in the original statement when it uses the verb *to be* or a **modal verb** (e.g. *can, must, will, would*):

I am happy.   *So am I. (I agree with your positive statement.)*

She's very kind.   *So are you.*

Grammar GPS

She *isn't* rich.	*Neither am I.* (I agree with your negative statement.)
He *isn't* very tall.	*Neither is she.*
He *was* sick.	*So was I.*
They *weren't* friendly.	*Neither were you.*
I *can* swim.	*So can I.*
You *mustn't* go there.	*Neither must you.*

We use the **auxiliary verb** in the original statement for all other verbs. If there isn't an auxiliary use the correct form of *do*.

I've *got* a cold.	*So have I.*
I *didn't* go out.	*Neither did we.*
They've *been* twice.	*So has Mary.*
She *understands* it.	*So does he.*
They *like* tennis.	*So do we.*

(BUT) I DO

When we make a statement which is the opposite of what the other speaker has said, we often use the elliptical form of the verb. (This means that some words are left out.) For example:

I'm really thirsty.	*I'm not.* (We don't say I'm not thirsty.)
I *love* eating fish.	*I don't.*
I *can* use this camera easily.	*I can't.*
I've *never* been here before.	*I have.*
He *didn't* buy anything there.	*I did.*

And to emphasise the opposite nature of the reply, we can add *but*, for example:

We *didn't* enjoy the film.	*But Mary did.*
I *want* to go to the sea tomorrow.	*But they don't.*

ALTHOUGH/EVEN THOUGH

These two words are used to indicate a surprising action we did or that happened. They can be used interchangeably.

Although/Even though it was cold, we went to the beach.
We went to the beach although/even though it was cold.

HOWEVER

However and *but* have the same meaning, but we tend to use *however* to start a new sentence.

Tom went to the new dentist's, but he wasn't happy with the treatment he got.
Tom went to the new dentist's. However, he wasn't happy with the treatment he got.

Note: a comma (,) always follows *however*.

UNIT 4

THE PRESENT SIMPLE PASSIVE and THE PAST SIMPLE PASSIVE: AFFIRMATIVE

We make the **passive voice** by putting the **main verb** of the active sentence into the **past participle** form and adding the verb *to be* in the same tense as the main verb was in.

Active voice	Passive voice
They *drink* tea all over the world.	Tea *is drunk* all over the world.
They *recycle* most of the bottles.	Most of the bottles *are recycled*.
He *found* this book in the street.	This book *was found* in the street.
They *made* these toys in China.	These toys *were made* in China.

If we want to show who did the action, then we add *by* + **the agent**.

My brother took these photographs.
These photographs were taken by my brother.

However, we do not usually put *by* + **the agent** when the subject of the active sentence is a personal pronoun such as *they* (*by them*) and *he* (*by him*) as in the four examples above.

THE PRESENT SIMPLE PASSIVE and THE PAST SIMPLE PASSIVE: QUESTIONS AND NEGATIVES

We form the interrogative and negative forms of the **passive voice** in the same way.

Active voice	Passive voice
Do you eat it hot or cold?	*Is it eaten hot or cold?*
Where *do they produce* these cars?	Where *are these cars produced?*
When *did they ban* cars here?	When *were cars banned* here?
What colour *did they paint* it?	What colour *was it painted?*
They *don't teach* English here.	English *isn't taught* here.
They *don't make* these clothes here.	These clothes *aren't made* here.
They *didn't show* this film.	This film *wasn't shown.*
The storm *didn't damage* the tents.	The tents *weren't damaged* by the storm.

MUCH, MANY and A LOT OF/LOTS OF

We use *much* with uncountable things and *many* with countable things.

How much information did you find out?	*I didn't find out much.*
How many apples did she buy?	*She didn't buy many.*
How much money did you collect?	*I didn't collect much.*

(Note: money is an uncountable noun!)

We can use *a lot of* (*lots of*) with both countable and uncountable things.

There were a lot of/lots of animals at the zoo. (countable)
There was a lot of/lots of rice in the store room. (uncountable)

We can also use *a lot* on its own.

How much water would you like?	*A lot, please.*
How many books has he got?	*A lot.*

FEW and A LITTLE

We use *few* with countable nouns and *little* with uncountable nouns. We often put a modifier like *very, so* and *too* in front of them.

There are too few books for the students. (countable)
She's got very few friends.
I had very little time to do it. (uncountable)
We took so little food with us.

CONSOLIDATION UNITS 3 and 4
FOR + THE PRESENT PERFECT and THE PAST SIMPLE

For often introduces a time phrase (e.g. *for a week, for years*). When such phrases are used with the **present perfect** they have a different meaning to when they are used with the **past simple**.

I have had a cat for two years.
(I bought the cat two years ago and I still have it.)
Tarek has been in our class for two months.
(Tarek joined the class two months ago, and he is still in it.)

Compare with:

I had a cat for two years.
(I had a cat for two years in the past, but I don't have one now.)
Tarek was in our class for two months.
(Tarek joined our class, stayed for two months, then left it.)

The same meaning occurs with the two tenses in questions.

How long have you lived in Doha?
(I know you still live there.)
How long did you live in Doha?
(I know you don't live there now.)

THE PRESENT PERFECT and THE PAST SIMPLE

In sequences of conversation about the past, talk often moves from the **present perfect** to talk about general things, to the **past simple** to talk about specific things.

Suzie: *Have you been to the shops?*
Lynn: *Yes, I have. Look what I've got.*
Suzie: *Wow! That T-shirt's great. How much did you pay for it?*
Lynn: *Only eight pounds.*
Suzie: *Lucky you! Were there many people in town?*

UNIT 5
CAN and BE ALLOWED TO

The verbs **can** and **be allowed** to are used interchangeably to talk about a situation in which permission is or is not given to do something.

We can take our mobile phones to school.
However, we can't/cannot use them in the classroom.
Can you use them inside the school buildings?

We're allowed to use the internet in the breaks.

They're not allowed to cycle in the school grounds.
Are you allowed to use calculators in maths exams?

In general, **be allowed to** is more formal than **can**. Also **cannot** is more formal than **can't**.

HAVE TO and MUST

We use **have to** in the affirmative and interrogative to talk about obligations imposed on us from outside. Look at these examples in the **present** and **past** tenses.

I have to write an essay for Monday.
What time does he have to arrive at school?
She had to pass her exams to get into university.

We use **not have to** to indicate a lack of obligation from outside.

We don't have to go to school tomorrow – it's a holiday.
I didn't have to wear a uniform at my primary school.

We use **must** in the affirmative to show self-imposed obligations.

I must see that new James Bond film!
You must read this book! It's really interesting.

In the negative, **must not** (**mustn't**) shows external rules.

You mustn't park here.
We mustn't run in the school.

MAKE and LET

We can use **make** in the construction *make somebody do something* to indicate that another person causes you to do something.

My friends made me take part in the competition.
John always makes us laugh.
Did he make you look at all his holiday photographs?

We use **let** to indicate that someone allowed or gave permission for us to do something.

They let us visit the museum although it was closed.
Did she let you borrow her CDs for the weekend?
Paul didn't let her see his paintings.

REFLEXIVE PRONOUNS: MYSELF, YOURSELF, etc.

The **reflexive pronouns** in English are made by adding **self** (singular) and **selves** (plural) onto the pronouns *my, your, him, her, it, our, them*. They usually occur as part of a fixed phrase (e.g. *to cut oneself, to hurt oneself*).

I can look after myself.
Are you angry with yourself?
He sometimes talks to himself.
It turns itself off after an hour.
We found ourselves in trouble.
It looks as though you didn't enjoy yourselves.
They were proud of themselves.

Note the singular **yourself** and plural **yourselves**.

EACH OTHER vs. OURSELVES, YOURSELVES, THEMSELVES

Look at the picture to see the difference between *each other* and *ourselves*.

They are introducing themselves.   They are introducing each other.

Look at these other pairs:

They're drawing each other. (drawing another person)
They're drawing themselves. (drawing a self-portrait)
We were angry with each other. (I was angry with you, you were angry with me.)
We were angry with ourselves. (We had both made the same mistake.)

These are some common phrases with **each other**:

Do you know each other?
We always help each other.
We haven't seen each other for months.
They didn't like each other.
My friends and I always give each other a birthday present.

Grammar GPS

WHO, WHICH and THAT

The relative pronouns *who* (for people) and *which* (for things) can both be replaced by *that*.

A conductor is a person who (that) directs an orchestra.
The police have caught the man who (that) robbed the bank.
I was shocked by the things which (that) they told me.
The house which (that) is next to mine was sold yesterday.

WHERE and WHEN

Where (to talk about place) and *when* (to talk about time) can be used as **relative pronouns**, as well as question words.

This is the place where he was last seen.
Do you remember the exact date when it happened?

BOTH and NEITHER

We use *both* to talk about two people (or two groups, two objects, etc) with positive reference, either by itself, or as *both of* + *pronoun*.

We both live in London.
Both of us live in London.
You are both responsible.
Both of you are responsible.
They both like football.
Both of them like football.

We use *neither* + *of* + **pronoun** to talk about two people (groups, objects, etc) with negative reference.

Neither of us plays squash.
Neither of you is strong enough.
Neither of them has ever been to America.

Note: the verb is always singular after *neither*, as it means 'not one person (singular) or the other person (singular)'.

UNIT 6
FIRST CONDITIONAL

We make the **first conditional** (sometimes called the 'real conditional') using two clauses, as follows:

If + **present simple** / *will* **future**

We use it to talk about situations that are real, related to future intended actions.

If it rains, I will stay at home.

We can also invert the two clauses, in which case there is no comma.

I will stay at home if it rains.
Where will you go if he leaves?

There are three types of negative sentences possible. The first two have the same meaning.

I will not (won't) go to the show if Mary goes.
I'll go to the show if Mary doesn't go.
I will not (won't) go to the show if Mary doesn't go.

MUST

In order to make the future of the verb *must*, we use the verb *will have to*.

Will you have to take the exam again if you fail?
We will have to work harder next year.

MAY/MIGHT and WILL

We use *will* to talk about definite facts in the future.

Chelsea will win the Cup.

We use *will* with an *if* clause to talk about future events which depend on certain conditions.

They will win if they do their best.

If we are unsure about the future outcome, we use *may/might*.

They may/might win.

If we use *will not/won't* we show that we think what we say is not possible.

People won't find life on other planets.

BE GOING TO

We use *be going to* to talk about future plans and intentions.

My best friend is going to study genetics.
They're going to build a new bridge next year.
I'm not going to take part in the competition.
What are you going to do if you don't get the job?

CAN AND COULD

We use *can* and *could* to ask questions; *could* is more formal and polite than *can*.

Can/Could you help me, please?
Can/Could I leave a message?

We often use *can* to talk about possibility if the verb in the main clause is in the present or present perfect tense.

She has installed Skype so she can make free video calls.
We use *could* if the verb in the main clause is in the past:
She installed Skype so that she could make free video calls.

SHALL

We use *shall* to ask a question, which is also a suggestion. It is followed by *I* or *we*.

Shall I get you something to drink?
Shall we come round later?

We can also use *shall* in genuine future questions, for example:

What shall I buy Tim for his birthday?
Where shall we go for our holiday next year?

Note: we are also asking for a suggestion.

IN ORDER TO and SO THAT

We use *in order to* and *so that* when we are explaining the reason for actions. The meaning of both phrases is the same, but the construction of the sentences is different.

I get up early so that I (can) have more time for breakfast.
I get up early in order to have more time for breakfast.
Hamid went to London so that he could learn English.
Hamid went to London in order to learn English.

We often use **can** to talk about possibility if the verb in the main clause is in the present or present perfect tense.

She has installed Skype so she can make free video calls.

We use **could** if the verb in the main clause is in the past:

She installed Skype so that she could make free video calls.

in order to + verb infinitive

The subject of the 'purpose clause' is the same as the subject in the main clause:

I caught the bus in order to arrive on time.
(= in order for me to arrive on time)
To make the negative form, write **not** after **order** and before **to**:

I caught the bus in order not to arrive late.

so/so that + *subject* + modal verb

With negative 'purpose clauses', you can use *have to* in its infinitive form after *didn't* to mean that something was not necessary:

She installed Skype so that she didn't have to pay for her calls.

Note: we use a normal verb, not a modal verb in negative purpose clauses.

The main clause can have a different subject to the 'purpose clause':

My dad's going to get a webcam so that we can see our cousins in Australia.

UNITS 5 and 6
VERB + PREPOSITION

Many verbs are followed by a particular preposition.

write to somebody
believe in something
think about something
wait for somebody
talk to somebody
look at something
laugh at somebody/something
die of something
apologise to somebody
listen to something/somebody

These four verbs have a different structure.

explain something to somebody
congratulate somebody on something
translate something into another language
prefer something to something else

And some verbs do not take a preposition.

phone/call somebody
influence somebody
enter something

When we make questions, the preposition goes at the end.

What does it depend on?
Who did the car belong to?
Which station were you listening to?
What did she thank you for?
What are you proud of?

PREPOSITIONS
IN

We use *in* with certain time expressions:

in May / in autumn / in 1995 / in the 21st century
in the morning / in the afternoon / in the evening

But we do not use *in* in these situations with **next** and **last**:

What are you doing next Thursday?
We moved to the country last year.

ON

We use *on* with certain time expressions:

on Monday / on 3 March / on your birthday / on that day

Notice these expressions:

in the morning / on Saturday morning
in the evening / on Friday evening

AT

We use *at* with certain time expressions:

at five o'clock / at half past seven / at New Year
at night
at the weekend

PHRASAL VERBS

Phrasal verbs are constructions with **verb** + **preposition** where the meaning is not literal. For example *go in* is not a phrasal verb, because it literally means to move inside a building or a room. Here are some phrasal verbs:

call somebody back (to return somebody's telephone call)
come from somewhere (to live in or be a native of a town or country)
look after somebody (to take care of somebody when very young, old or ill)
make up with somebody (to repair damage in a relationship and become friends again)

IN, *INTO*, *OUT* and *OUT OF*

These prepositions are of place and movement.

There was a ball in the pool. (place)
I jumped in to get the ball. (with *jumped*, movement)
I jumped into the pool. (with *jumped*, movement)
I couldn't get out. (with *get*, movement)
I couldn't get out of the pool. (with *get*, movement)

These prepositions are opposites:

in	out
into	out of

Grammar GPS

ON, OFF, UP and DOWN

These prepositions are of place and movement.

I hung a picture on the wall. (place)
I took the picture off the wall. (with *take*, movement)
I fell off my bike. (with *fall*, movement)
We walked up the hill. (movement)
We ran down the stairs. (movement)

The prepositions often form part of a **phrasal verb**:

get on / get off the train
put on / take off a jacket
turn up / turn down the volume
prices go up / go down

UNIT 7
INDIRECT SPEECH

When we are reporting what someone said, we can make our text more interesting by using different **reporting verbs** instead of just using **said** all the time. Useful verbs are: *ask / invite / order / remind / want / warn / tell* somebody (*not*) *to do something.*

I asked my friend to walk me home.
My friends invited me to stay with them for the weekend.
I reminded my brother not to use my computer.
The police ordered everyone to leave.
Paul wants me to sing in his band.
He warned us not to tell anyone.
My parents told me to clean my room again.

INDIRECT QUESTIONS

As with **indirect speech**, there are different structures we can use when reporting questions which make the text more interesting than just using *asked* all the time.

Direct question	Indirect question
Where is the nearest bus stop?	Could you tell me where the nearest bus stop is?
When does the film start?	Do you know when the film starts?
How did it happen?	I want to know how it happened.
Is Paul coming with us?	They want to know if Paul is coming with us.
Does she speak English?	Do you know if she speaks English?
Have you ever played this game?	Can you tell me if you've ever played this game?

UNIT 8
WOULD

The construction *would* + **infinitive without to** is used to talk about future situations where the speakers express their ideas of the probabilities and possibilities, usually with some kind of condition related to the situation.

I would prefer to go home. (If there were an opportunity.)
Would you help a situation like that? (If you were in that kind of situation.)
She wouldn't take a risk. (If she was in that kind of situation.)
We wouldn't know what to do. (If we were in that situation.)

They'd pay for your trip. (If you asked them, or if you decided to go.)
Note the contraction (*'d*) in the final sentence.

SECOND CONDITIONAL

The **second conditional** is also known as the 'unreal' conditional, because it is a way of making a hypothesis about future actions. The two clauses are formed as follows:

If + **past simple** / *would* + **infinitive without** *to.*

Either of the two clauses can be first, but **if** the *if-* clause comes first, we put a comma (,) after it.

If I didn't know the way, I'd ask someone.
I'd ask someone if I didn't know the way.

We can also put the negative form in either or both of the clauses. The first two sentences here have the same meaning; the third is different.

If it rained, I wouldn't be happy.
If it didn't rain, I would be happy.
If it didn't rain, I wouldn't be happy.

Note: we also use this form for giving advice, using the fixed phrase *If I were* + **pronoun**.

If I were you, I'd see a doctor.
If I were him, I'd change my job.
What would you do if you were me?

We can make questions and answers like this:

Sam:	*What would you do if you won the lottery?*
Jim:	*I'd buy a house by the sea.*
Paul:	*How would he react if we told him about it?*
Bill:	*He'd be very surprised.*
Jane:	*If you were in trouble, who would you ask for help?*
Phil:	*I'd ask you.*

VERY, REALLY, QUITE and A BIT

We use *very, really, quite* and *a bit* in front of an adjective to modify its strength. *Very* is the strongest, and *a bit* is the weakest.

These mountains are very dangerous.
The exam was really difficult.
Mariam is quite strong.
That path looks a bit dangerous.

A LOT, MUCH and A BIT

We use *a lot, much* and *a bit* in front of a comparative adjective to modify its strength. *A lot* is the strongest and *a bit* is the weakest.

The film is a lot better than the book.
This restaurant has become a lot more expensive.
I'd like to be a bit taller.

Grammar GPS

IN CASE

We use the phrase *in case* to talk about making plans for a possible future situation.

Bring something to eat in case you get hungry.
Why don't you take your umbrella in case it rains?
You should take some money in case you want to buy something.

Note: the verb which follows *in case* is in the present simple.

OR

As a conjunction, *or* is used to introduce a negative consequence if the action suggested is not taken.

We have to leave early, or we'll miss the train.
Take a phrasebook with you, or you won't be able to communicate.
You should buy the tickets today, or you'll have to queue tomorrow.

Note: the verb in the *or* clause is in the *will* future.

UNLESS

The conjunction *unless* is used to introduce a clause which tells us what needs to happen to avoid a negative situation.

You'll miss the bus unless you hurry up.
We'll have to take a taxi unless your dad gives us a lift.

Note: the verb in the **unless** clause is in the **present simple**, while the verb in the other clause is in the **will future**.

This construction is an alternative for the first conditional. We could say the two examples above as follows, with the same meaning:

You'll miss the bus if you don't hurry up.
We'll have to take a taxi if your dad doesn't give us a lift.

CONSOLIDATION UNITS 7 and 8

MY and MINE

We can talk about possession using possessive adjectives (*my, your, her...*) or possessive pronouns (*mine, yours, hers...*), and also using the saxon genitive (*'s / s'*).

This is my mobile.	*This mobile is mine.*
Is this your bag?	*Is this bag yours?*
These are his jeans.	*These jeans are his.*
This is our classroom.	*This classroom is ours.*
Are those their clothes?	*Are those clothes theirs?*
This is Hani's house.	*This house is Hani's.*

IT + BE

We can use *it* + *be*, mostly in the form of *it's*, to present many situations in everyday speech.

It's a camera.
It's nice here.
It's five kilometres to the airport.
It's time to say goodbye.

This also works in the **past simple**.

It was a beautiful day.

LIKE

We can use the word *like* when we want to make a comparison to show similarities between two people, two things or two actions.

He cooks like a professional chef.
Some vegetables, like peppers and broccoli, contain a lot of vitamin C.

When we talk about the similarities in appearances we use **look like**.

My mum looks like her mother.
Do you look like your brother?

We can also use it to talk about behaviour, character or actions of people and things:

What is he like?
You ate one of those cakes. What was it like? (What did it taste like?)
What did the team play like?

Note the difference in meaning in these two exchanges, and the different verbs used before *like*.

John: *What is Tom like?*

Pete: *He's nice, but a bit silly sometimes.*

John: *What does Tom look like?*

Pete: *He's short and slim.*

Note: do not confuse these meanings of *like* with the frequently used verb *to like*.

John: *What does Tom like?*

Pete: *He likes sport and computer games.*

Infinitive	Past simple	Past participle
be	was / were	been
become	became	become
begin	began	begun
bite	bit	bitten
blow	blew	blown
break	broke	broken
bring	brought	brought
build	built	built
burn	burnt (or burned)	burnt (or burned)
buy	bought	bought
catch	caught	caught
choose	chose	chosen
come	came	come
cost	cost	cost
cut	cut	cut
do	did	done
draw	drew	drawn
drink	drank	drunk
drive	drove	driven
eat	ate	eaten
fall	fell	fallen
feel	felt	felt
find	found	found
fly	flew	flown
forget	forgot	forgotten
get	got	got
give	gave	given
go	went	gone
grow	grew	grown
have	had	had
hear	heard	heard
hurt	hurt	hurt
keep	kept	kept
know	knew	known
learn	learnt (or learned)	learnt (or learned)
leave	left	left

Infinitive	Past simple	Past participle
lend	lent	lent
light	lit	lit
lose	lost	lost
make	made	made
mean	meant	meant
pay	paid	paid
put	put	put
read	read	read
ride	rode	ridden
run	ran	run
say	said	said
see	saw	seen
sell	sold	sold
send	sent	sent
sing	sang	sung
sit	sat	sat
sleep	slept	slept
speak	spoke	spoken
spell	spelt (or spelled)	spelt (or spelled)
spend	spent	spent
stand	stood	stood
stick	stuck	stuck
swim	swam	swum
take	took	taken
teach	taught	taught
tell	told	told
think	thought	thought
throw	threw	thrown
understand	understood	understood
wake	woke	woken
wear	wore	worn
win	won	won
write	wrote	written

Notes

Notes

English Insights Student's Book 1

Helen Stephenson and Jane Bailey

Publisher: Gavin McLean

Commissioning Editor: Carol Goodwright

Marketing Manager: Michelle Cresswell

Project Editor: Tom Relf

Production Controller: Elaine Willis

Art Director: Natasa Arsenidou

Cover design: Andrew Oliver and Vaisilki Christoforidou

Text design: Maria Papageorgiou

Compositor: Q2AMedia services Pvt. Ltd.

National Geographic Liaison: Leila Hishmeh

ISBN: 978-1-4080-6812-0

National Geographic Learning
Cheriton House, North Way, Andover, Hampshire, SP10 5BE
United Kingdom

Cengage Learning is a leading provider of customised learning solutions with office locations around the globe, including Singapore, the United Kingdom, Australia, Mexico, Brazil and Japan. Locate our local office at **international.cengage.com/region**

Cengage Learning products are represented in Canada by Nelson Education Ltd.

Visit National Geographic Learning online at **ngl.cengage.com**
Visit our corporate website at **www.cengage.com**

Photo credits
The publishers would like to thank the following sources for permission to reproduce their copyright protected photographs:
Cover photo: l (Cameron Spencer/Getty Images), c (Jody Macdonald Photography), r (Hans Berggren/Johnér Images/Corbis)
pp 1 l (Cameron Spencer/Getty Images), c (Jody Macdonald Photography), r (Hans Berggren/Johnér Images/Corbis), 5 (Keren Su/Corbis), 6 l (digitalskillet/iStockphoto), c (Shutterstock), r (Ashwin82/iStockphoto), 8 cr (Adrian Sherratt/Alamy), br (EmmanuelD/Fotolia), 12 c (Medford Taylor/National Geographic Image Collection), bl (Penny Tweedie/Corbis), br (Marnie Burkhart/Fancy/Getty Images), 15 (Shutterstock), 17 (vaskoni/iStockphoto), 18 tr (Art Directors & TRIP/Alamy), b (Denise Truscello/Getty Images), 20 bl (Michael de Plaen), bc (Benjamin Harte), br (courtesy of Alexander Prior), 21 bl (Sipa Press/Rex Features), tr (Rex Features), 24 c (Penny Tweedie/Alamy), bl (courtesy of Farsad Labbauf), br (Shutterstock), 25 tr (Alexander Burkatovski/Corbis), br (Chris Hellier/Alamy), 32 tr (Pitt Rivers Museum), cr (Pitt Rivers Museum), 33 (Pasieka/Science Photo Library), 34 cr (Mark Thiessen/National Geographic Image Collection), br (Norbert Wu/Minden Pictures/Getty Images), 36 (LeggNet/iStockphoto), 37 (cristianl/iStockphoto), 39 (Vidura Luis Barrios/Alamy), 40 tl (David Evans/National Geographic Image Collection), bl (powderkeg stock/Alamy), br (Mooneyphoto/Malaria No More/Press Association Images), 45 (Tom Pfeiffer/Alamy), 46 (Nickolay Khoroshkov/Fotolia), 49 (Shutterstock), 51 (David Hughes/Fotolia), 52 cl (Raveto07/iStockphoto), bl (Jeremy Richards/iStockphoto), br (littledutchgirl/iStockphoto), 53 (Reuters/STR New), 54 (Michael Nichols/National Geographic Image Collection), 60 bl (Yves Gellie/Corbis), br (Lucasfilm Ltd/Paramount/The Kobal Collection), 61 (Juanmonino/iStockphoto), 62 cr (Shutterstock), cl (herkisi/iStockphoto), br (Shutterstock), 64 bl (Laoshi/iStockphoto), br (wrangel/iStockphoto), 67 (WinterWitch/iStockphoto), 68 b (Shutterstock), cl (Jean Gill/iStockphoto), 69 (Picture Contact BV/Alamy), 73 (Mark Thiessen/National Geographic Image Collection), 74 (Paramount Television/Kobal), 76 bl (Karen Kasmauski/National Geographic Image Collection), br (Reuters/Issei Kato), 80 c (Harveys Art/Fotolia), cr (Hodder & Stoughton), br (2000adonline.com), 88 tr (World Religions Photo Library/Alamy), cr (Robert Preston Photography/Alamy), 89 (Shutterstock), 90 cl (AP/Press Association Images), c (Shutterstock), cr (WPA Pool/Getty Images), 92 tc (itanistock/Alamy), tr (Shutterstock), 96 tl (Greg Ward/iStockphoto), tr (Douglas Fisher/Alamy), 97 (The Prince's Trust), (jimkruger/iStockphoto), 101 (Jim Zuckerman/Corbis), 102 cr (Jon Arnold Images Ltd/Alamy), br (Paul Sutherland/National Geographic Image Collection), 103 (Borge Ousland/National Geographic Image Collection), 104 (Joanne Zh/Dreamstime), 105 (M. Sobreira/Alamy), 108 cl (Cotton Coulson/National Geographic Image Collection), bl (LTuray/iStockphoto), br (Brian J. Skerry/National Geographic Image Collection)

Illustrations by Mark Draisey pp 35, 63, 116, 120, 122 (cl); Celia Hart pp 30, 109, 113 (cl); 114; Martin Sanders (Beehive Illustration) pp 12, 32, 40, 52, 68, 80, 96, 108; Eric Smith pp 19, 29, 57, 69, 75, 79, 85 (tr); 86 (tl); 113 (t), 117 (tr), 119 (tr, br), 121 (tl), 122 (tr), 128; Laszlo Veres (Beehive Illustration) pp 41, 43, 58, 81, 85 (br), 86 (cl), 117 (tl, bl), 118 (tl), 121 (tr), 122 (tl), 123

The publishers would like to thank David A. Hill for his contribution to this book.

Printed in China by RR Donnelley
1 2 3 4 5 6 7 8 9 10 – 16 15 14 13 12